# Library Web Site Policies
## CLIP Note #29

*Compiled by*

**Jeri L. Traw**
Coastal Carolina University
Conway, South Carolina

College Library Information Packet Committee
College Libraries Section
Association of College and Research Libraries
A Division of the American Library Association
Chicago 2000

The paper used in this publication meets the minimum requirements of American National Standard for Information Sciences–Permanence of Paper for Printed Library Materials, ANSI Z39.48-1992. ∞

**Library of Congress Cataloging-in-Publication Data**
Traw, Jeri L.
    Library Web site policies / compiled by Jeri L .Traw.
        p. cm. -- (CLIP note ; #29)
    Includes bibliographical references.
    ISBN 0-8389-8088-0 (alk. paper)
    1. Library information networks. 2. Library information networks--United
States--Management. 3. Web sites--Management. 4. Web sites--United
States--Management. 5. World Wide Web.  I. Association of College and Research
Libraries. College Library Information Packet Committee. II. Title. III. CLIP notes. ; #29.

Z674.75.W67 T73 2000
021.6'5--dc21

                                                                    00-030633

Printed on recycled paper.

Printed in the United States of America.

04 03 02 01 00        5 4 3 2 1

# TABLE OF CONTENTS

**Policy Manual**

# CLIP NOTES COMMITTEE

Lewis R. Miller, Chair
Butler University Libraries
Indianapolis, IN

Roxann Bustos
Reese Library
Augusta, GA

Jody L. Caldwell
Drew University Libraries
Madison, NJ

Doralyn H. Edwards
Fondren Library
Rice University
Houston, TX

Jamie Hastreiter
William Luther Cobb Library
Eckerd College
St. Petersburg, FL

Jennifer Taxman
Lucy Scribner Library
Skidmore College
Saratoga Springs, NY

Mickey Zemon
Emerson College
Boston, MA

# INTRODUCTION

## OBJECTIVE

The purpose of this College Library Information Packet (CLIP) Note is to study the characteristics of library web site policies and to provide small college and university libraries in need of such policies the tools to develop them. This study does not attempt to critique these policies but serves to document current practices smaller academic libraries are using to help manage their web sites. The basic premise of this CLIP Note is "to share information among smaller academic libraries as a means of facilitating decision making and improving performance" (Morein 226).

## BACKGROUND

As a web site grows, so do the responsibilities and burdens. The number of files seems to multiply every few months, and the demands for additional content come from a million different directions. This constant demand and work load leave little time for a sole administrator or web team to prepare policies that give web sites direction and that establish roles and responsibilities of participants in the production process.

No matter what page users might visit on a site, they should be able to understand the layout and navigational structure. A well-organized and visually consistent site helps users feel comfortable and less intimidated by the vastness or complexity of a site. Implementing a consistent design strategy facilitates easy access to information and establishes a recognizable, unified visual identity. Web policies aid in achieving these goals.

Web site policies not only benefit users but are also of great importance to those designing the pages. Policies help new and even experienced web authors work creatively within a framework to produce meaningful and accessible content. Having structural and design guidelines available from the start, web authors are freed to deal with the more critical issue of producing meaningful content for users. This is especially true for newcomers to web authoring.

Policies to govern the design, content and basic maintenance of a library web site are very important to the overall success of a site. Successful library web sites are well designed, easy to navigate, and help users quickly locate needed information. Often, written policies that address these issues are not thought about until a library finds itself with a site that does not function well, is hard to navigate, and/or needs redesigning.

## SURVEY PROCEDURE

Standard CLIP Note procedures were used to undertake and complete this survey. An initial proposal and draft of a survey instrument were submitted to, reviewed, and approved by the CLIP Notes Committee of ACRL's College Libraries Section. The instrument was based on a model for health science libraries. (Lingle) Surveys were sent to 224 small university and college libraries that agreed to be part of CLIP Notes surveys. In addition to completing the questionnaire, many responding libraries gave permission to include their web site policies in this book.

## SURVEY RESULTS

A total of 163 surveys were returned for a response rate of 73%, which suggests that the research on this topic is important to college librarians. Only 3 libraries indicated they currently do not have a web site. Of the 160 libraries with web sites, only 25% returned surveys that responded to all the policy questions. The completed surveys breakdown as follows: 78% returned by libraries with written policies, 17% with informal (non-written) policies, and 5% without any policies. Twenty-one percent of the libraries with web sites indicated they have written policies to govern their sites.

### General Information  (Questions 1 - 9)

Questions 1 through 9 of the survey gather basic information about the libraries being surveyed. A majority of 68% indicate their institutions are private, while libraries at public institutions represent only 31%. The average student FTE at the responding institutions is 2,921, ranging in size from 643 to 8,487. They employ an average of 8 full-time librarians, 12 paid staff members, and 16 student assistants. Based on the data provided for the most recent IPEDS (Integrated Post-secondary Education Data System) Report, the responding libraries have average expenditures of: $509,380 on Information Resources, total for all categories; $29,713 for electronic books, serial backfiles, and other electronic materials; and, $68,746 on current electronic serial subscriptions and search services. Electronic resources account for 19% of the total Information Resources expenditures for the responding libraries.

### Web Site Information: General Information  (Questions 10 - 11)

Question 10 establishes that 98% of those responding have web sites. The 2% without a web site indicate one is in the planning stage. Responses to Question 11 show that 68% of libraries with a web site have sites older than 2 years, 23% have been created within the last 1-2 years, and 9% have existed for less than one year.

**Web Site Information: Responsibility  (Questions 12 - 17)**

To understand the importance of having library web site policies some background on the nature of the responsibilities associated with the creation, maintenance, and day to day running of the web site is essential. Questions 12 through 17 present an interesting picture of how the responding libraries administer their sites.

Overall web site responsibility has remained constant with 57% responding that responsibility has not changed hands since site creation.  Regardless of title, small college library web sites appear equally administered by a single person or web master and a team/committee or group of individuals.  A comparison of the overall FTE staffing numbers with the number of personnel involved in web page creation indicates that for many only a small handful are participating in web work.

Most of the respondents indicate their web site is loaded on the Institution's server (81%) as opposed to a library server (13%).  For most this is not a problem because the library is allowed to load its pages directly to the institution's server (85%).  The job of loading library web pages appears to be relatively controlled. Only 4% of the libraries indicate that anyone from the library can load pages.  The most common job title of persons creating library web pages is Reference/Public Services librarian.

**Web Site Policies: General Information  (Questions 18 - 26)**

A little over half the libraries surveyed (52%) indicate that their institution has policies to govern the college/university's web site.  A much smaller percent (21%) indicate their library has developed policies specifically for the library's web site.  For a large portion of this group (42%) their written policies are still in the draft stage; and roughly one-third (36%) have only informal, non-written policies.  The most common reason given for not having policies (27%) is that library needs are currently being met by their institution's policies.

The task of writing web policies appears typically to involve a library web team/committee (45%) and is not always performed at the same time the web site is created (54%).  The majority (67%) indicate their policy development occurred within the past year or is currently in progress, and was spurred on by a web site redesign project. Only 26% of the reporting libraries with policies created them at the outset. As far as re-writing or evaluating their policies, most libraries report doing so on an irregular basis.  For some, their policies are too new to need a re-evaluation.

Questions 23 - 26 shed light on how the libraries themselves regard their policies and the actual web sites.  Most policies begin with a mission/purpose statement that establishes the need for the policy and importance of the issue it addresses. A significant number of the library web policies (67%) include a mission or purpose statement. Another indicator of a policy's importance is whether or not it is followed. Only 5 responding libraries indicate not adhering to their policies. Interestingly, a total of 58% of the libraries surveyed make their policies available to the public either via the web or in print.

Question 26 sparked the most responses. Thirty-eight out of the forty libraries who completed the entire survey, as well as an additional 25 libraries, indicate they view their web site as an extension of existing services. These 25 additional respondents represent libraries without web site policies, but they felt strongly enough about the role of their web site that they read the entire survey and chose to answer this one question. The majority of respondents (76%) believe their library's web site is an extension of existing services, primarily: reference, library instruction, interlibrary loan, and reserves.

## Web Site Policies: Characteristics (Questions 27 - 33)

The final section of the survey offers insights into the key characteristics associated with library web site policies. Specific types of pages or resources most commonly addressed by responding libraries are, in rank order: departmental pages, collection development of Internet resources, and professional and personal pages. Also mentioned as important are subject guides and bibliographies, library instruction materials, and Internet bibliographies (webliographies).

Ninety percent of respondents characterized their policies as design and content oriented. Procedural/technical (51%) or philosophical/administrative (44%) are also common characterizations. Less common characterizations were policies that address site maintenance (38%) or performance issues (21%).

The most typical design and content issues addressed are:

- the use/standardization of headers and footers
- navigational elements
- date files are updated
- format/type of information to include
- indication of page authorship

The most commonly included procedural/technical elements are:

- submission and contribution procedures
- spell checking and proofreading for errors

- testing pages prior to uploading
- web browser compliance
- server access

Policies more administrative in nature were also identified as important. Typically they include:

- Site responsibilities
- Web site mission
- Target audience
- Scope of the site
- The administrative structure

Maintenance issues are less commonly addressed but still drew a significant number of responses. The more frequently addressed issues are: the link checking and repair process; maintenance responsibilities/assignments; the process for updating pages; reporting site problems; and the issue of routine site maintenance and backups.

Performance related issues are not commonly addressed, receiving the fewest responses of any of the policy characteristic questions. However, the most often covered issues are: performance of pages in various browsers and their versions; file size of images and load speed; broken link reporting; site backup plan; and, file size of pages and load speed.

## Conclusion

Library web site policies are a relatively new idea for most small college and university libraries, and with more of these libraries creating and redesigning existing sites their use and importance will continue to grow. They range from simple mission statements explaining the overall philosophy of the library web site to detailed manuals that govern the philosophy, development, creation, and maintenance in greater detail. These policies provide assistance to those involved in web page development and creation, fostering creativity while enabling the web site to develop around a common set of standards. With this in mind, libraries currently without any policies should consider developing them prior to undergoing any major site redesign or in the event that additional personnel participate in development.

## Selection of Documents

The policies reproduced in this CLIP Note were selected to illustrate the variety of policies small college and university libraries are using to manage their library web site. To highlight the different types presently used, the policies are grouped by type: mission statement, collection development, and full policy manual.

# Selected Bibliography

Anderson, Mary Alice. "Developing Web Page Policies or Guidelines." <u>Technology Connection</u> 4 (1997): 16-7.

Braun, Linda W. "Libraries and Internet Policy." <u>Internet Trend Watch for Libraries</u> 1.2 (July 1996): n.p. Available: http://www.itwfl.com/policy.html. 15 May 1998.

Braun, Linda W., and Jennifer Fleming. "From the Desktop: Editors' Note." 1.2 (July 1996): n.p. Available: http://www.itwfl.com/july96.html. 15 May 1998.

"Guidelines for Web Document Style & Design." http://sunsite.berkeley.edu/Web/guidelines.html. 1 May 1998.

Lingle, V.A., and E.P. Delozier. <u>World Wide Web and Other Internet Information Services in the Health Sciences: a collection of policy and procedure statements</u>. MLA DocKit. 7. Chicago: Medical Library Association, 1996.

McClements, Nancy, and Cheryl Becker. "Writing Web Page Standards." <u>College & Research Libraries News</u> 57 (1996): 16-7.

McGowan, J.L. "Creating an Institutional Web Presence." <u>Information Outlook</u> 1.11 (1997): 18-21.

Morein, P. Grady. "What is a *CLIP Note*?" <u>College and Research Libraries News</u> 46 (1985): 226.

Rauch, Ellen. "Library Policies: getting ready to write." <u>Internet Trend Watch for Libraries</u> 1.2 (July 1996): n.p. Available: http://www.itwfl.com/writepol.html. 15 May 1998.

Shedlock, J., D.C. Barkey, and F. Ross. "Building the Electronic Health Science Library for the Twenty-First Century: the Galter Library experience." <u>Medical Reference Services Quarterly</u> 15 (Winter 1996): 1-12.

Swab, J.N., M.E. Thompson, and S. Rose. "NAL Home Page on the World Wide Web." <u>Agricultural Libraries Information Notes</u> 22 (Jan./March 1996): 1-6.

Sylvan, Peter. "Website Design Guidelines for Public Libraries." http://www.tiac.net/users/mpl/guidelines.html. 5 June 1997.

Wuolu, David. "World Wide Web Publishing: creating a policy statement." <u>World Wide Web Publishing: An Overview</u>. http://indigo.lib.lsu.edu/general/part1.html. 1 May 1998.

# CLIP Note Survey Results

# CLIP Note Survey: Library Web Sites and their Policies

## General Information  (Questions 1- 9)

1.    Institutions:          163 responses        74% response rate


2.    Is your Institution:   Public          31%          (51)
                             Private         68%          (111)
                             No Response      1%          (1)


Number of full-time equivalent (FTE):

3.    <u>Students enrolled</u>

           average:  2,921      range:  536 – 7,520        153 responses

4.    <u>Librarians</u>

           average:  8        range:  1 – 32              161 responses

5.    <u>All other paid staff</u>

           average:  12       range:  1 – 47              159 responses

6.    <u>Student Assistants</u>

           average:  16       range:  1 – 100             158 responses


Expenditure Amounts:

7.    Information Resources: total for all categories:  (IPEDS Lines 12 – 19)

           average: $509,380                    158 responses
           range:    $10,831  -  $2,570,033


8.    Books, serial backfiles, and other materials:  Electronic (IPEDS Line 13)

           average: $29,713                     132 responses
           range:    $0  -  $625,197

9. Current serial subscriptions and search services: Electronic (IPEDS Line 15)

        average: $68,746           148 responses
        range:    $0 - $943,300

## Web Site Information: General Information (Questions 10 - 11)

10. Does your library have a web site?

| 163 responses | 98% | YES | (160) |
|---|---|---|---|
| | 2% | NO, planning stage | (3) |

11. How long has your library web site been in existence?

| 160 responses | 9% | less than 1 year | (14) |
|---|---|---|---|
| | 23% | 1 – 2 years | (37) |
| | 68% | longer than 2 years | (109) |

## Web Site Information: Responsibility (Questions 12 - 17)

12. Who is currently responsible for (in charge of) the content of the library's web site?

| 160 responses | 33% | team / committee | (53) |
|---|---|---|---|
| | 31% | library web master | (49) |
| | 36% | other: | (58) |
| | | (specify position) | |

        57%    Single individual    (33)
        -Public Services Librarian
        -Reference Librarian
        -Electronic Services Librarian
        -Serials Librarian
        -Director
        -Head of Automation
        -Systems Librarian
        -Head of Reference

        43%    Group of people    (25)
        -all Librarians
        -Publications Committee
        -Team/committee & web master
        -Library Systems Unit
        -Web master & computer services

12a.   Has this changed since the site was first created?

159 responses

|       |                             |       |
|-------|-----------------------------|-------|
| 43%   | YES                         | (68)  |
| 57%   | NO, same since the beginning. | (91)  |

13.   Where is your site loaded?

160 responses

|       |                       |        |
|-------|-----------------------|--------|
| 13%   | library's server      | (21)   |
| 81%   | institution's server  | (130)  |
| 6%    | other:                | (9)    |

-- (7) split, some on library's and some on institution's
-- (1) Biology Department server
-- (1) Communication Department server

14.   Can your library upload its pages directly to the server?

160 responses

|       |                            |        |
|-------|----------------------------|--------|
| 85%   | YES                        | (136)  |
| 14%   | NO, no direct access to server. | (22)   |
| 1%    | NO, other reasons:         | (2)    |

--some we can load, others not
--at this time it is done by a third party contracte[d] by the
  college

15.   Who is responsible for uploading the library web pages to the server?

159 responses

|       |                            |       |
|-------|----------------------------|-------|
| 4%    | anyone from the library    | (7)   |
| 30%   | only the library web master | (47)  |
| 49%   | select library personnel   | (78)  |
| 13%   | other                      | (21)  |
| 4%    | [chose multiple answers]   | (6)   |

16.     How many people create pages for the library web site? (Specify numbers)

Librarians

average:  4          range:  1 – 24          144 responses

Library staff

average:  2.4          range:  1 – 10          67 responses

Student workers (in the library)

average:  2          range:  1 – 7          33 responses

Non library personnel

average:  2          range:  1 – 5          19 responses

17.     Please list job titles of those persons who create web pages for the library:

Top 10 job titles are:

--Public services/Reference librarian                  77 responses
--Systems librarian                                    30 responses
--Head/Coord. of Reference/Public Services             28 responses
--Dean/Director/University librarian                   26 responses
--student worker/assistant/technician                  21 responses
--access/electronic services/resources librarian       20 responses
--circulation supervisor/head of circ.                 16 responses
--technical services librarian                         14 responses
--library technical assistants/associates              13 responses
--librarians                                           13 responses
--administrative assistant/secretary                   11 responses
--government documents librarian                        11 responses
--Assoc./Asst. Dean/Director/Univ. Librarian           11 responses
--cataloging librarian                                 11 responses

## Web Site Policies: General Information  (Questions 18 - 26)

18.    Does your college/university have any policies, guidelines, style manuals, or procedures to govern the development, creation, and maintenance of web pages?

159  responses

| | | |
|---|---|---|
| 49% | YES | (78) |
| 3% | YES, [can't give out] | (5) |
| 38% | NO | (61) |
| 9% | I do not know. | (15) |

19.    Does the Library have any written policies, guidelines, style manuals, or procedures to govern the development, creation, and maintenance of web pages?

160 responses

| | | |
|---|---|---|
| 11% | YES | (18) |
| 9% | YES, draft stage. | (14) |
| 1% | YES, [can't give out] | (1) |
| 36% | [Informal, nothing written] | (58) |
| 9% | [Needed, no time or info.] | (14) |
| 27% | NO, [no need at this time] | (43) |
| 7% | NO, other reasons | (12) |

20.    When were the library's web site policies written?

39 responses

| | | |
|---|---|---|
| 26% | before/as web site was created. | (10) |
| 20% | during [web site's 1st year] | (8) |
| 54% | at some other time: (When?) | (21) |

--under development/ in process of formulating
--in the past eight months
--last 6 months
--2 years after creation of site
--during the summer of 1998

21. Who wrote your web site policies?      (Check all that apply)

38 responses

| | | |
|---|---|---|
| 45% | library web team / committee | (17) |
| 10.5% | someone else in the library | (4) |
| 10.5% | someone outside the library | (4) |
| 13% | [selected multiple answers] | (5) |

someone else in the library: (Who?)

--Department heads
--Electronic services librarian with input from other librarians
--Library publications committee
--Reference librarian, reviewed & approved by committee

someone outside the library: (Who?)

--Computer services department
--Computer services, librarians were not allowed to
   participate

22. Have your policies ever been re-evaluated and/or re-written?

35 responses

| | | |
|---|---|---|
| 3% | YES, on a regular basis | (1) |
| 66% | YES, on an irregular basis | (23) |
| 31% | NO. Our reasons are: | (11) |

--Informal evaluation & changes
--Who knows?
--They are new
--We are just now doing them
--Too early to make an evaluation
--Policy will be reviewed by the web committee as needed

23. Does the policy include a mission statement or statement of purpose?

36 responses

| | | |
|---|---|---|
| 33% | YES | (12) |
| 67% | NO | (24) |

24.  Do you feel the library's web site policies are adhered to?

37 responses

| | | |
|---|---|---|
| 49% | YES | (18) |
| 38% | For the most part, but not always | (14) |
| 13% | NO | (5) |

25.  Are these policies available to the public from the library's web site?

36 responses

| | | |
|---|---|---|
| 33% | YES they are. | (12) |
| 8% | On the [web, access restricted] | (3) |
| 17% | Not on web, but available | (6) |
| 42% | NO, they are not available | (15) |

26.  Does the library consider its web site a service?

38 responses

| | | |
|---|---|---|
| 26% | YES, a separate service | (10) |
| 74% | YES, extension of existing services: | (28) |

Check all that apply:

| | | |
|---|---|---|
| 68% | Reference | (26) |
| 58% | Interlibrary loan | (22) |
| 39% | Reserves | (15) |
| 66% | Instruction | (25) |
| 34% | Other: | (13) |

--collection development
--circulation
--library information
--acquisitions
--government documents
--special collections
--extended/distance education
--cataloging
--periodicals
--systems
--audiovisuals
--extension of all library services

## Web Site Policies: Characteristics  (Questions 27 - 33)

27. Do your library's web site policies touch on the following issues specifically?
    (Check all that apply)

    34 responses

    | | |
    |---|---|
    | collection development for Internet resources | 16 |
    | personal pages of library personnel | 6 |
    | professional pages of library personnel | 9 |
    | library departmental pages | 24 |
    | other: (e.g. subject guides & bibliographies) | 21 |

28. Characterize your web site policies:      (Check all that apply)

    39 responses

    | | |
    |---|---|
    | philosophical / administrative in nature | 17 |
    | design and content oriented | 35 |
    | covers procedural / technical matters | 20 |
    | addresses site performance issues | 8 |
    | concerned with site maintenance issues | 15 |
    | other: | 3 |

29. The procedural and administrative issues addressed by the library's web site
    policies include:     (Check all that apply)

    32 responses

    | | |
    |---|---|
    | web site mission | 14 |
    | target audiences | 14 |
    | scope of the site | 14 |
    | the administrative structure | 14 |
    | site responsibilities | 19 |
    | training roles / responsibilities | 7 |
    | other: | 6 |

30. The design and content issues addressed by the library's web site policies
    include:      (Check all that apply)

35 responses

| | |
|---|---|
| use / standardization of headers and footers | 24 |
| HTML standards | 16 |
| format and type of information to be included | 21 |
| resource evaluation and selection criteria | 15 |
| sample templates, forms, scripts, etc. | 15 |
| standards for fonts, color, graphics size and type | 19 |
| web page length | 8 |
| use of style manuals (i.e. Chicago, Yale, Sun, etc.) | 5 |
| navigational elements | 22 |
| indication of date files are updated | 22 |
| indication of page authorship and contact info. | 21 |
| other: | 6 |

31. The procedural / technical issues addressed by the library's web site policies
    include:      (Check all that apply)

29 responses

| | |
|---|---|
| available training and support information | 5 |
| URL creation standards (file naming conventions) | 6 |
| testing pages prior to uploading | 13 |
| submission and contribution procedures | 15 |
| spell checking and proofreading for errors | 14 |
| inclusion of ALT attribute for images | 6 |
| server access | 7 |
| web browser compliance | 13 |
| other | 4 |

32. The performance related issues addressed by the library's web site policies
    include:      (Check all that apply)

    23 responses

    | | |
    |---|---|
    | file size of page, and speed they should load | 6 |
    | file size of images, and speed they should load | 10 |
    | performance of pages, various browsers and versions | 13 |
    | disaster recovery plan | 4 |
    | site backup plan | 6 |
    | broken link reporting procedures | 10 |
    | other: | 1 |

33. The maintenance related issues addressed by the library's web site policies
    include:      (Check all that apply)

    32 responses

    | | |
    |---|---|
    | link checking and repair process | 17 |
    | reporting of site problems | 13 |
    | process for updating pages | 16 |
    | maintenance responsibilities / assignments | 17 |
    | routine site maintenance and backups | 8 |
    | site evaluation process | 6 |
    | site re-design process | 6 |
    | other | 5 |

# Web Site Policies

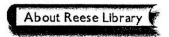
Methodology of this Web Site:

This site was created with the following principles in mind:

- Shorter screens are preferable.
  Site users should have to go no more than 3 levels deep to reach the material they seek.
  We seek to be responsive to our library users. It should be possible to make comments to the library from every screen.
  Speed is important to our users.

If you find violations of these principles, please contact <u>Jeff Heck</u>, Automation Librarian.

ASU Home    Search ASU    Directory    News and Events    What's New    Contact ASU Webmaster

Contact Reese Library Webmaster

Last modified on: Wednesday, September 22, 1999 10:45:29

## Besse Library Web Site Vision Statement

The purpose of the Ralph M. Besse Library Web Site is to support the mission of the library in its endeavors to meet the information needs of Ursuline College students, faculty, and staff by providing Library services in a World Wide Web environment.

DRAFT DRAFT DRAFT DRAFT DRAFT DRAFT DRAFT DRAFT DRAFT

## Williams College Library Web Page Mission Statement
### (work in progress)

The Williams College Library exists to support the curricular, research, and informational needs of Williams College students, faculty and staff. To do so, the Library selects, acquires and preserves materials across formats and provides access to them in three ways: (a) through direct links to all types of electronic resources, including, but not limited to, online subscription journals and databases, CD-ROMS, and selected Web sites; (b) through systematic organization (e.g., cataloging, indexing), (c) through effective instruction in the evaluation and use of these resources.

To these ends, the Library's Web Page will have three purposes:

1. to provide electronic access to library collections, licensed subscription databases, e-journals, selected Web sites, librarian-produced guides and other appropriate information sources [part "a" above]

2. to provide intellectual access by serving as a teaching tool for the Williams College community to promote the full and effective use of all available resources [parts "b" and "c"] above

   The Library's Web Page is not intended to be a substitute for the personal and individualized reference and research assistance that has traditionally been associated with Williams College Library. While every effort will be made to include as much detail as possible in Web-published guidelines and instructions, the Library's Web Page is not intended to be a comprehensive guide to Library collections, electronic or print.

   Activities in this area include but may not be limited to:

   - creation of or linking to Web documents which help the user identify, locate, and use print and other types of Library resources in selected subject areas

   - creation of or linking to Web documents which aid the user in any aspect of research, especially the creation of or linking to Web documents which help the user identify, access and evaluate Internet-delivered resources

   - creation of or linking to Web documents which facilitate the effective searching and retrieval of information in any database to which the Library provides access

03/11/99

3.  to provide information to Williams College students, faculty, and staff, Williamstown residents, and the wider academic community about the Library's organization, services, policies and activities

    - "organization" includes:
        directory information, including e-mail and home page links
        library department descriptions of functions

    - "services" include:
        circulation
        interlibrary loan
        reference and research help
        workshops and classes
        faculty services

    - "policies" included relate to:
        circulation collection development (future)
        interlibrary loan
        other school groups' use of Library resources
        Williams College Network access
        Government Documents

    - "activities" include:
        special library programs (such as the Williams Writers' Series)
        community outreach

    - "resources" include:
        FRANCIS
        e-journals
        news sources
        library statistics
        computer labs

03/11/99

# Selection Criteria:
# Internet Resources by Academic Department

## Scope:

Internet resources selected for this page support academic departments and programs at Amherst College. The emphasis is on metasites, databases, indexes, reference sources, collections of online journals, related academic associations, etc. The category of "course related" can include more narrow websites that wouldn't meet the above criteria but support the curriculum. Pages linking to resources in print and electronic on given topics are also appropriate. Generally, individual monographic equivalents or individual journal titles are not linked from these pages.

## Quality:

High quality, stable sites that support the curriculum and augment the traditional collection are selected. A closer look is taken at sites that are not .edu, .gov, or .org. Coherent organization of information and ease of navigation within the site are important. The library strongly prefers sites with good accessibility coding, including alt text tags and no frames options. Individual selectors will check site links from recommended pages to make sure that they are (mostly) good, active links. Generally, the date of last update should be included on all sites selected.

*last update: 11/24/98*
*Comments regarding this page should be directed to: <u>Susan Edelberg</u>*

## *WORLD WIDE WEB*

### *INTRODUCTION*

*Fitchburg State College Library maintains a Home Page on the World Wide Web to:*

- *provide information about the Library*
- *provide an online reference service*
- *provide access to the Library's catalog and paid online services/subscriptions*
- *meet the general informational and educational needs of the College community*

*This policy is consistent with the existing Collection Development Policies and the Library's goals and objectives for service to the College community.*

### *INFLUENCING FACTORS*

*Information about the Library is compiled by the Library Director and representatives of the various Library departments.*

*Online inquires are handled by Reference Librarians as part of regular reference service.*

*Links to World Wide Web sites from the Library Home Page are selected to broaden, enrich, and complement the Library's print and non-print collections. Sites are evaluated according to their credibility, quality, and usefulness in order to support the needs and interests of the Library's patrons and staff.*

*Selection of World Wide Web sites is based on reviews and recommendations in sources such as Internet World, Online, and Library Journal.*

*Evaluation of sites is based on such factors as:*

*Access*
- *Stable site*
- *How fees, if any, are paid*
- *Consistently available*

*Design*
- *Well organized*
- *Clear instructions*
- *Easy to use*
- *Uncluttered and cleanly designed*
- *Graphics that enhance the content*

*Content*
- *Authoritative*
- *Documented, accurate, verifiable*
- *Timely and updated regularly*
- *Preference given to educational, governmental, and non-profit organizational sites*

■ *Appropriateness of subject matter*

## DEVELOPMENT PLAN

*The Fitchburg State College Library Home Page will continue to change in response to the ever-changing nature of the Internet. The Home Page should not grow beyond the number of links which can be maintained in a timely manner.*

## RETENTION AND WEEDING

*Linked sites are reviewed periodically for access, design, and content. If a site no longer meets our selection criteria, or is inactive or out-of-date, it is removed.*

 *Forward Comments and Suggestions to Library Director*

*Revised: August 19, 1999*
*Best if viewed with Netscape or Microsoft Explorer*

Note: These documents represent current policy and practice, however, they are subject to change and revision without notice.

WORLD WIDE WEB "READING ROOM"
COLLECTION DEVELOPMENT POLICY STATEMENT
Draft version - modified 10 February 1999

1. Criteria for inclusion of a site:
   a. Utility as a research tool
   b. Accuracy of information presented
   c. Precision/focus of subject matter
   d. Currency of information
   e. Probable permanence of site
   f. Commercial sites included?
      i. If useful information is available at no charge
      ii. If the information available is not biased or inaccurate
      iii. If advertising is not overly abundant or aggressive
   g. Hotlink lists especially desirable?
      i. Somebody else already did the work
      ii. However, we have no quality control over the contents
   h. Links to sub-sections of an already-cited web site:
      i. Should only be included if they are especially noteworthy
      ii. Link should be embedded in the annotations for the main site's listing rather than in its own listing

2. Organization and display of Reading Rooms
   a. Conceptual organization
      i. Arranged in sub-categories by subject matter (or format, e.g. hotlink lists, e-zines?)
      ii. Little to no duplication of sites between sub-categories--consider a "general resources" sub-category if warranted
   b. Visual display
      i. Head of site: table (?) of sub-category headings with jump links to each subcategory section
      ii. Sub-category section headings as <H3> headers
      iii. Individual entries as alphabetical list within sub-categories
3. Individual site listings
   a. Listing title should be as close to a verbatim quote as is reasonable (minus "Welcome to...", etc.) of either:
      i. <TITLE> of web page, or
      ii. the major page header
   b. Each listing should be annotated briefly
      i. no more than a line or two
      ii. name of the site sponsor/originator if known
      iii. brief site description
      iv. no value judgments
   c. Special designations (custom bullets?) for:
      i. hotlink lists
      ii. different sponsor types
         (1) commercial
         (2) government
         (3) university
         (4) professional organization
         (5) individual

# HTML Style Sheet

These guidelines represent our goals for consistency throughout the www.amherst.edu/~library site. Due to the dynamic nature of the Web, changes to this guide are likely. We strongly urge library web developers to review this style sheet frequently.

1. Directory names should start with caps (but not be all caps), ex:

   ~library/public_html/Online

2. File names should start with lower case, ex:

   ~library/public_html/Online/govedocs.html

3. Both directory and file names should be as short as possible while still being explicit (try to avoid multiple words linked by underscores),ex:

   use "newfile.html" rather than "new_file.html"

4. If you're making major edits of a file directly in UNIX space using an editor other than emacs, save a copy of the file first so that you can use it later to recover in case of damage to the file you're editing. (Ex: cp xxxx.html xxxx.save, then edit xxxx.html.) Be sure to remove yoiur save file(s) once you've finished your editing to reduce confusion between file versions.

5. All HTML files should end in .html rather than .htm.

6. All HTML files should be reviewed not only for appearance and functionality in a browser (preferrably in both Netscape MSIE) but for clarity and ease of editing with either emacs or vi.

7. All HTML files prepared by other people in your behalf should be reviewed closely by you and LERG for content and by Jan for HTML usage/functionality/correctness.

8. When you are creating/testing new files, it's a good idea to work on them in a Temp or InDev subdirectory of your workspace (or in your personal UNIX space). Ask Jan for help hiding files in these directories from Web search engines, if that's important to you.

9. Every file/page should contain a datestamp and "statement of responsibility" at the end of the file/page. The simplest way to do so is to add the following lines to each file:

```
<p>
<!-- Footer -->
<i>
<font size=-1>
last update:  mm/dd/yy
<br>
Comments regarding this page should be directed to:
<a href="mailto:xxxx@amherst.edu?Subject=[URL or title of pa
provider's name]</a>
</font>
</i>
<!-- End Footer -->
</body>
</html>
```

10. All text in all HTML files should be left-aligned.

11. If you use other than emas, vi, or Notepad to create your HTML, make sure you save your files as "text only" or "text only with line breaks" so that the file doesn't not become one long, uneditable, line in UNIX.

12. Create your files so that they have only one HTML tag per line, if at all possible, as in the example at #9 above.

13. Files should be made accessible as possible to users employing non-graphical browsers such as Lynx. Specifically, all references to images should include "alt" tags, text-only versions of graphics-heavy pages should be maintained, and <noframes> elements should be included in frames-based files.

14. Files should conform to ADA guidelines.

*last update: 12/18/98*
*Comments regarding this page should be directed to: Jan Jourdain*

**Bowdoin College Library     Draft Style Sheet**

Download the printable version using Adobe Acrobat

### *For Department and Individual Documents on the Library Web*

A "Library Style", or standard set of visual cues, helps users maneuver through the pages we produce, identifies each page as part of a larger unit, and can save staff time and effort. This style sheet has been developed to guide library staff who design and maintain web pages for public use.

Departmental and staff pages not designed for the public, such as internal policy and procedure manuals, may follow different guidelines.

The design elements should be used on any page linked directly to the Library Web (that is, the Library Home Page, or any Library page that can be reached in a single step.) Beyond that, we urge you to follow the design elements as appropriate. Please follow the performance and maintenance standards throughout your web document, unless the standards are incompatible with the document's purpose.

| Home | Web Style | Draft Style | Timeline | Webmaster Resources |

**Return to Top**

### All Web Pages linked to the Library Web Gateway should share these elements:

*Design Elements*

- All Library Web Pages should use the basic banner design. (Basically a thin, fast-loading title graphic at the top with "Bowdoin College Library" somewhere on it). This can be in a smaller font than the other title information you put on the banner. The Library Web Master can provide a template and instructions and may be able to help alter the banner template to fit your specifications.
- Use Section Heading Bars and Shortcut links if you like. If you do use them, they should be similar enough to the Library Gateway page to be easily recognized by a new user.
- Place a button on the bottom banner that will lead users back to your first-level page. Your first-level page should have a button that takes the user back to the Library Gateway page. The Web Master will provide the first part of the bottom banner and the library gateway button.
- Other navigational buttons are optional, but we recommend that you use no more buttons than can be placed on one line.
- Fonts, when used as part of graphical elements such as banners and buttons, should be selected for clarity and high contrast with the chosen background. We recommend using Anti-Aliased fonts, a technique used to smooth outer edges of the letters and enhance their appearance. The banner on the Library Gateway page is Ariel MT Rounded Bold.
- Choose background and text colors that provide a sufficient level of contrast, but also harmonize with each other.
- If you wish to use a background image, chose one that does not compromise the performance or legibility of your pages on various browser. We urge you to consult with the Web Committee if you plan to include backgrounds or other large images.

- images that carry significant meaning, such as buttons and banners, define meaningful alt tags, to give the user a clue to their importance in case they fail to load properly.

*Basic Performance Elements*:

- First- and Second-Level pages should each fit on one screen. We suggest that these be no more than 600 pixels wide, so that all the information will fit on smaller monitors.
- Images should never be more than 256 colors (8 bit). It is strongly suggested that images be 16 colors (4 bit).
- Avoid designing tables more than 500 pixels wide.
- Test your pages on older Mac and Windows computers. The public labs still have some Mac II's and Windows machines with 386 processors. Lower quality monitors measure less than 14" and have screens of 640 x 480 pixels.
- Under average local conditions, our page should take no more than a minute to load. Add up the kilobytes required for all the images on each page. Try to keep it to less than 30 kB per page.
- If your pages are likely to be used frequently by people off-campus, try to test your work on other browsers, and an older version of CIS-supported browsers.

*Maintenance Elements*:

- Pages should include the date created, and the date of last (significant) revision of content or function. It is suggested that these dates be placed at the bottom of the page.
- The name and e-mail address of the page developer should also be on the page. The e-mail address should be an active link. Again, we suggest that this information be placed at the bottom of the page.
- Page developers must commit to keeping page content up to date. It may be appropriate to allow some documents to become dated, but this should be a conscious decision, subject to later review.
- Counters can't be relied upon to collect accurate statistics. If you want to use a counter, make sure you state when you began counting, and be sure to reset at appropriate intervals.
- The Library Web Master must have full access to all pages s/he or the Web staff are expected to update, or may be reasonably expected to update in the near future.
- After you've published your web pages, be sure to make an announcement to the whole library staff. For other suggestions on publicity, contact the Web Committee.Pages should include the date created, and the date of last (significant) revision of content or function. It is suggested that these dates be placed at the bottom of the page.

---

---

## Courtright Memorial Library

### Web Page Policy & Guidelines

## I. Purpose:

The library's mission is to support the teaching and research needs of the Otterbein community by facilitating access to information and materials. The library's web site will support this mission by providing web-based research instruction and information.

The system librarian is the designated Webmaster. The Webmaster will work with members of the Web Governing Group (WGG), all library units, and appropriate college agencies to keep the web site current and useful.

## II. Responsibility for Development and Management of Pages

Staff development of information resources on the Library's web page should be encouraged throughout the library. Identification of ideas for pages and resources to be made available from staff, actual development of the pages, and maintenance of those pages needs to be distributed widely in the following manner:

Top Level Page(s) - the Web Governing Group (WGG) is responsible for regularly reviewing the effectiveness of the top level pages in terms of the overall categorization of information, appearance, etc. It also monitors development at all levels of the Libraries' WWW presence and makes recommendations for improvement in content, design, and maintenance of these pages.

Department and Unit Pages - The various departments and liaison librarians are encouraged to develop pages that focus on the interests and needs of their particular users. The Webmaster and the WGG are responsible for designating staff to manage the overall content and design of these pages.

## III. Content:

Library web page content will support the mission of Courtright Memorial Library.

The web links selection is part of the library collection development. The selection criteria specified in the Library's Collection Development Policy should apply to the web links selection. These links are to be maintained by the page designer or by the responsible unit. Authors should check their pages monthly to make sure links are operational, the information is up to date and appropriate to the Library's mission.

Changes in library policies, staff, hours and services should be forwarded to the Webmaster for posting on the web site. These posted policies, hours and services should be reviewed at the beginning of each quarter to verify accuracy.

## IV. Style and Restrictions:

1. It is important for the web site to have a consistent design format, so that users can easily identify when they are on library-created pages. Some units may choose to follow a different style; if so, the style should complement the other pages and be applied consistently.

2. Titles in a <TITLE> tag should be meaningful and be no more than 64 characters in length. Title words are used by many web search engines to index documents. The information in the <title> tag also becomes the bookmark entry when saved by users The web site should also have meaningful headings to clearly identifies the document. Many search engines weight the relevance of the document retrieved based on words in the headings. Using descriptive headings takes advantage of this feature.

3. All capitals should generally be avoided at all unless used with acronyms, initialisms, or abbreviations.

4. A table of contents is recommended for documents longer than 4 screens long when viewed on an average computer system. An average computer system is defined as any Macintosh or IBM compatible with a 14 inch monitor displaying 256 colors at a resolution of 640x480. Pages should also be no more than 10 screens long when viewed on an average computer.

5. Pages which supposedly or actually are under construction should not be activated for use until enough construction has been completed to provide something useful. If the page is included, it should be clearly labeled as "Not yet active," and the link should not be activated.

6. Personal home pages that has nothing to do with the library services will not be linked to the Library's web pages. Useful documents for librarian and staff in pursuit of their professional duties can be linked to an internal web site for easy access to.

7. Each page should avoid duplicating documents that appear elsewhere on the server or on the Internet. Instead, link to them.

8. Each subset of pages should provide a contact name and -e-mail link for the person responsible for the page(s). Otherwise the Webmaster's name and e-mail link will be provided. Each page must include link back to the Library's Home Page.

## V. Adding New Pages:

New web pages to be added to the web site should be directed to the Webmaster who will review them with the Web Governing Group within the context of the entire web site, and for compliance with the Web Policy.

The Webmaster will have the responsibility for transferring appropriate pages and also make needed changes to existing Unit and other pages.

Once a page has been linked to the Library's site, the URL (i.e.: file name and directory) should not be changed unless absolutely necessary.

## VI. Changing Existing Pages:

Simple updates and date changes can be reported to the Webmaster.

Substantial changes involving content or style should follow the same process as "adding new pages." The Webmaster, the Web Governing Group reserve the right to remove pages that do not conform to the Library Mission and the Web Policy.

## Milne Library Web Site Policy

Statement of Purpose:

The library web site will provide an electronic gateway to information and research sources that support the college's academic programs. In addition, the site will provide links to satisfy other information needs of SUNY College at Oneonta students, faculty, and staff. The web site will be logically organized, attractive, and easy to use, and will include accurate and up-to-date information and links. It will be designed and maintained in accordance with the standards established by the college.

1) There will be a Web Advisory Committee which will meet as necessary to consider larger issues of policy, design, functionality, and content.

2) There will be a web coordinator who oversees the maintenance of the web site.

3) Library web pages will conform to the SUNY Oneonta web guidelines, which are available at:

http://www.oneonta.edu/ocs/policies/webpolicy.html.

4) Library web pages will follow the style guide from the college, which is available at:

http://www.oneonta.edu/ocs/policies/webpolicy.html.

5) Library web pages will use standard HTML avoiding proprietary (browser specific) ~ML.

6) Library web pages will follow a uniform layout and appearance. The web coordinator will make templates available for page design at http://www.oneonta.edu/~libweb/templates .

7) Each page will have an assigned individual responsible for its content. Library web pages must be reviewed on a regular basis. Dead links should be checked promptly when reported.

8) Graphics should be used in a conservative manner.

9) Personal web pages should be made through university provisions for personal pages. Information on personal web page creation is available at:

http://www.oneonta.edu/ocs/documentation/web_html/homepage.html.

10) Library web pages will observe copyright law.

11) All pages will link back to the main library page as well as the college main page.

12) Page maintainers are encouraged to point to college department pages where appropriate. Collaborations with other college departments regarding web pages is encouraged.

13) This document is subject to periodic review and revision.

2/27/98

**Trinity University          Elizabeth Huth Coates Library**

Home    Research    Internet    IMS    Databases    QUEST    Services

# Library Web Guidelines

Purpose / Scope / Audience / Administration / Submitting documents / Web team members / Additional resources

### Statement of purpose:

The library's web pages have several purposes. The primary purposes are to enhance the library's instructional support, expand the library collections to include electronic information on the internet, and provide information about the library. The specific content will include: (1) Reference Resources (2) Internet Help which includes evaluative instruction on internet research (3) Instructional Media Services (4) Electronic Resources including subject guides (5) Services and Forms which include public service policies and forms available on the web and (6) Library Information, general information about the library.

### Scope

The web pages are intended to include information and links to information on research, information resources, forms and information for services, and informational documents about the library and Instructional Media Services and their units.

### Primary audience:

The primary audience of the library web pages is students, faculty and staff of Trinity University. Other audiences include other information seekers, including others in the library profession, as well as other professionals.

### System Administration:

**The library web pages are administered by a library web team appointed by the library director. The library web team will represent all divisions within the library.**

**The web team is responsible for:**
- **The overall organization of the library web site.**
- **Designing and maintaining the home page and the first page of each of the main subdivisions of the site.**
- **Designing a template page for all subsequent pages.**
- **Maintaining a consistent and easy-to-use web site for the Library.**
- **Transferring all pages into the Library Web Server.**
- **Coordinating with the University Computer Center on matters of hardware, software and technical issues for managing the web pages.**
- **Reviewing all pages, primarily for making appropriate linkages.**
- **Preparing a site index.**
- **Maintaining standard file names on the server.**

**The web team will not be responsible for reviewing content, but will review pages to determine appropriate linkages to other pages.**

Document Submission:

The web team encourages the library professional staff to submit documents for inclusion in the library web site. Authors should first contact the web team member responsible for the area of content of their proposed page. These web team members can provide guidance and editing assistance. It is the responsibility of the web team member to review and transfer the page to the library web server and to make all appropriate links to other pages.

It is suggested that a general style manual be consulted before beginning to work on a page. Documents should be concise, if possible, and graphics should only be used if they provide images that help explain or demonstrate the subject of your document. Also, plan to consult with the web team member assigned to your area. It is their responsibility to review and then add your web page to the library page and to make all appropriate links.

**Individual authors will be responsible for:**
- Determining the content of their pages, including all links.
- Using Microsoft Word for a document created with a word processor.
- Using Microsoft Front Page as the editor for creating HTML documents.
- Contacting the appropriate web team member for assistance and for help submitting documents to him/her for downloading.
- Providing index terms to be added to the web site index and suggestions for linkages to other pages.
- Maintaining the content and links on their pages. This includes reviewing them periodically to ensure links are accurate, then providing updates to their pages.

The web team has created a template to be used for all pages. An author may choose to use the template when creating HTML documents and must clear the use of all graphics with their web team member. The template will be kept in the common folder for the library on TUCC/12.

The web team members have been assigned specific sections of the library web site to manage. Please consult the appropriate team member for assistance.

**The web team members are assigned as follows:**
- Chris Nolan and Carol Gill will work with Reference, Interlibrary Loan, Documents and Special Collections
- Donna Hernandez and Ruby Miller will work with Technical Services, Collection Development and the Front Office
- Ruby Miller will work with Circulation/Access Services
- Denise Amos will work with Instructional Media Services

## Additional Resources:

The following is a resource that includes some useful hints as well as additional resources for creating web pages.

Libweb Document Guidelines, San Diego State University.
ANU - Quality, Guidelines & Standards
University of Maryland Library's Style Guide for Authors of Web Pages
University of Wisconsin's Campus Libraries Web Page Standards and Guidelines
Lewis-Clark State College's style guide

Also see our Site Index for more information.

http://www.trinity.edu/departments/library/webguide.html
Last updated on January 24, 2000
Send comments to The Library WebTeam

# the utc Lupton Library
# WEB WORKS

## GUIDELINES FOR THE DESIGN AND CONTENT OF UTC LIBRARY WEB PAGES

Each of the UTC Library's web pages should contain the following information:

1. One of the standardized UTC Library headers such as:

   - Book Works
   - Instruction Works
   - Journal Works
   - Media Works
   - Service Works
   - Staff Works
   - Web Works

2. One of the standardized UTC Library footers, including:

   - The date of the page's last revision
   - The name, email address and mailto link of the page's author
   - The name, address, and phone number of the UTC Library
   - A link to the UTC Library's Information Page (LUPTON.HTML)
   - A copyright statment
   - A link to the UTC Home Page (WWW.UTC.EDU)

3. One of the standardized UTC Library page templates, including:

   - Coordinated background colors or image files
   - Coordinated text, link, and visited link color schemes for page links
   - Coordinated font type, size, and color schemes for page text
   - Coordinated font type, size, and color schemes for page section headings

Most UTC Library web pages should also contain:

1. Navigational links to the major sections of longer pages
2. Navigational links to the top of longer pages

## NOTES ON WEB PAGE DESIGN

Web page **designers should**:

- Keep the layout simple and intuitive
- Use a consistent layout across all related pages

- Organize pages so readers can quickly scan for information
- Group related information semantically (using organization)
- Group related information visually (using headings or rules)
- Create pages that can exist independently of other pages
- Write clearly and concisely
- Spell check and proofread each page
- Use images that are relevant to the UTC or UTC Library's site/organization
- Design for low-end PC's and slow connections
- Posterize or delabelize all images
- Use dimensionality

Web page **designers should not**:

- Overuse text emphasis (boldface, italics, or underlines)
- Use heading tags for emphasis
- Use blinking or glowing text for emphasis
- Clutter a page with unnecessary images
- Link to irrelavent pages
- Underestimate the importance of navigation aids
- Underestimate email as a communication tools
- Use terminology/tags specific to one particular browser
- Use a technology for its own sake

Web page **designers should remember** that:

- The first page is the most important page!
- Nothing communicates better than the written word!
- A web page is fundamentally different than a printed page!
- Take advantage of the unique characteristics of the medium!
- Content is king!
- Keep your content up-to-date and fresh!
- Register your site with the major web indexes and directories!

## NOTES ON WEB PAGE VIEWING

The pages on the UTC Library's web server are designed to be viewed on a 17"
computer screen with web browsers using the following font settings:

```
Normal text............11 pt proportional font

Header1 text..........18 pt proportional font

Header2 text..........16 pt proportional font

Header3 text..........14 pt proportional font

PREformated text....... 9 pt fixed font

All other text........11 pt proportional font
```

## NOTES ON WEB PAGE CONTENT

The UTC Library's web server contains the following types of files:

- Files with an **.html** extension (web browser required)
- Text files with an **.txt** extension (web browser required)

- Image files with a **.gif** extension (web browser required)
- Image files with a **.jpg** extension (web browser required)

- Files with a **.doc** extension (MS Word viewer required)
- Files with a **.pdf** extension (Acrobat reader required)
- Files with a **.pm6** extension (PageMaker viewer required)
- Files with a **.ppt** extension (Powerpoint viewer required)
- Files with a **.xls** extension (MS Excel viewer required)

The UTC Library's web server does not contain:

1. Copyrighted materials in any form without the expressed, written consent of the original copyright owner
2. Images (i.e. photographs, paintings, videos, movies, or other derivatives thereof) or recordings of people without their expressed, written consent
3. Commercial, for-profit advertisements in any form
4. Confidential information
5. Any images or data which would be abusive, profane, harrassing or sexually offensive to the average person

Even though the Manager of the UTC Library's Web Server reserves the right to remove or refuse any document, graphic, audio, form, program, or data file which does not comply with the above guidelines, page authors should be aware that they are are ultimately responsible for what they post on the UTC Library's server.

Any infringement of applicable copyright laws and any posting of obscene, harrassing or threatening materials on the UTC Library Web Server may be in violation of local, state, national or international laws and can subject the page authors to litigation by the appropriate law enforcement agency.

## NOTES ON COPYRIGHT

**WARNING TO DESIGNERS**: Copyright law restricts what information can be placed online. Page authors may not copy, post, distribute, or resell copyrighted information without the expressed, written consent of the copyright holder.

**WARNING TO VIEWERS**: Much, but by no means all, of the information available on the Internet is not copyrighted and free.

Much of the of the free information on the Internet is contributed by individual academics, hobbyists, researchers, or computer scientists. While much of this information is valuable, much of it is self-published and tends to go out of date very quickly. Moreover, much of it also can be filled with errors and misinformation.

Some of the free information is contributed by the government. The government's Internet information corresponds very closely to printed government information and is usually very reliable and up-to-date.

Much of the remaining information which is posted on the Internet is produced by businesses and is copyrighted. Some copyrighted information has been illegally posted on the Internet without the permission of the copyright holder.

When in doubt, it is best to assume that material is copyrighted!

## UTC GUIDELINES FOR THE DESIGN AND CONTENT OF WEB PAGES

- UTC Style Guidelines
- UTC Design Guidelines

## OTHER GUIDELINES FOR THE DESIGN AND CONTENT OF WEB PAGES

- Web Style Guide by Tim Berners-Lee
- Yale University's Web Style Guide

---

This page was last revised on 07/01/99 by a UTC Cybrarian.

The UT Chattanooga Lupton Library is located on Vine Street in Chattanooga, TN (1-423-755-4506).

WELLESLEY COLLEGE LIBRARY
Guidelines for "Library" and "Internet" CWIS Directories

These guidelines are intended to permit orderly co-ordination of the CWIS pages provided by the library.
- Joan Stockard (rev. 12/98)

1. BACKGROUND

    (a)  LIBRARY directory                   http://www.wellesley.edu/Library/

       - Files are those concerned with library services and collections plus some
        provided by the library for other areas of CWIS.

    (b)  INTERNET directory               http://www.wellesley.edu/Internet/

    - Files are primarily "Internet resources for.... " pages

NOTE about graphics files

    - Each of the 2 main directories includes a SUB-directory called Gifs

        \*\*\* ALL TYPES OF GRAPHICS FILE ARE PLACED IN 'GIFS'; none
         should be in INTERNET or LIBRARY file sequence

2.  EDITING AN EXISTING PAGE

    - Alert the co-ordinator about your editing plans \*in advance\*
      so that any possible directory/filename/links ramifications can be anticipated.

    - Please do your editing by downloading the page to your own
      machine or a diskette (Download with: WinsocFTP or Fetch)

    - When editing is completed and tested, replace page on server AND:

        (a) Notify co-ordinator

           \*ESSENTIAL - so that change will be backed up!

        (b) Replace printout of page in the MASTERS notebook
          in the R&IS Office

        (c) E-mail to the CWIS webmaster a short description
          of  the revision for the WHAT'S NEW listing on
          the CWIS and in other publicity.

SPECIAL EDITING NOTE FOR FULL-TEXT JOURNALS

        If you linking to a specific full-text journal licensed to the Library and cataloged by
        the Library  (Ex.: journals in JSTOR, Project Muse. OR individual e-journals)

    - Be sure to mention:

(a) "For Wellesley users only"
(b) Provided by a Library subscription

- If necessary, mention

(a) Adobe Acrobat Reader required
(b) AA Reader available on College's public file servers

- For EXAMPLES, see "Internet Resources for..." English or Math

---

## 3. ADDING NEW PAGES

- Alert the co-ordinator to your plans well IN ADVANCE so that
any possible directory/file name ramifications can be anticipated.

  : If needed, co-ordinator will create a SUB-directory

- Work out with cc-ordinator where new page(s) will link to the
library-provided CWIS menus.

- Co-ordinator will provide a FILE NAME for your page that will
harmonize with the existing files in the Library or Internet
directory.

  : REMEMBER that graphics file will go in subdirectory called Gifs.

  - To avoid filename duplication, check that subdirectory before
choosing a filename for your graphic.

- When new page completed... and tested.... and on server

(a) Notify co-ordinator

   ESSENTIAL!  Co-ordinator will update our backup Zip disc!

(b) Pencil in filename(s) on directory list in
MASTERS notebook in the R&Is office

(b) Put printout of page in appropriate place in
the MASTERS notebook

(c) E-mail to the CWIS webmaster a short description
of the new page(s) for the WHAT'S NEW listing
on the CWIS and in other publicity.

js:cwis-guidelines.txt

# Web Guidelines for Cornette Library

---

| Web Page Construction Home | Web Design Advice Home |

## A few words about consistency

To maintain visual consistency at the Cornette Web site, we have provided several basic templates, making use of HTML 4.0 transitional (the most recent HTML standard - you can learn more about HTML 4.0 transitional by going to: http://www.w3.org/TR/REC-html40/). The templates are located in the Web Templates folder on the P drive. The templates are best used in a word processing program such as Microsoft Word. Please note that Web authors are not obliged to use them. However, Web authors are expected to follow the style guidelines below, whether they use the templates or not. Note that any deviations from the guidelines must be approved by the Webmaster.

Return to top.

Web authors are welcome to create Cascading Style Sheets in lieu of using HTML 4.0 transitional, however, they are responsible for ensuring that the pages can be viewed and printed across browsers and platforms. Finally, for all Web pages you produce we strongly encourage you make the extra effort, and validate those pages as HTML 4.0 transitional. You can do this by going to http://validator.w3.org. Validating pages as HTML 4.0 transitional will ensure high quality HTML coding, and cross platform/browser compatibility.

Return to top.

## Design Requirements

### All pages need to contain Meta Tags:

The title area of all Web documents must include meta tags as shown here:

```
<head>
<title>Cornette Library Sample Page </title>
<meta name="Author" Content="your name">
<meta name="Updated" Content="date of revision">
<meta name="Description" Content="whatever description best
describes your page">
```

*<meta name="Keyword" Content="whatever keywords best
describe your page">*
</head>

Return to top.

## All pages need to contain a statement of responsibility:

A statement of authorship/last revision will be provided in the following format:

> West Texas A&M University, Cornette Library
> Authored by page author, job title. E-mail:
> youraddress@mail.wtamu.edu **(optional)**
> Comments to the Web Task Force **(optional)**
> All contents copyright (c) 1998, WTAMU. All rights reserved.
> Last revised: June 2, 1998.
> URL of the page

Return to top.

## Where appropriate add an electronic Reference link:

Add the following link on pages where a link to reference services is appropriate:

> Any questions? Please feel free to send an electronic information
> request to reference@mail.wtamu.edu.

Return to top.

# Look and Feel Requirements

All pages must consist of:

- a white background
- black body text
- maroon, navy, green, fuchsia, slate blue, purple, black or brick headers (see templates)
- visited links - which will be gray and underlined
- unvisited links - which will be navy blue and underlined

Return to top.

# Navigation Requirements

- All unit home pages must contain a link to the library home page.

- Unit pages must provide a link back to the unit home page.
- Pages more than three screens in length must provide "top" links (top links reduce scrolling since the user, by clicking, returns to the top of the page).

Return to top.

# Access Requirements

Please bear in mind that pages will be accessed by a variety of users, many of whom have limited bandwidth and computing power. As such, please adhere to the following:

- All pages making use of tables or making extensive use of graphics should be made available in a text and/or non-tables version.
- Graphics must be fewer than 30KB and must include alt, width, and height attributes. Whenever appropriate, provide a thumbnail of large images. In the case of photographic images, using millions of colors, try to use JPEG as often as is possible since this format will provide the smallest file sizes for this type of image. Simple images like drawings, logos and so forth are best saved as GIF. Optimally, GIF images should be interlaced.
- Color is rendered differently over varying browsers and platforms. In situations where you will be choosing colors for your pages (remember that background must always be white; however, you may wish to select sections of text and so forth in a color of your choosing), be sure it is one of the 216 colors which can be viewed both on the Windows and Macintosh platforms. For more information go to:

  http://www.lynda.com/hex.html or
  http://home.rica.net/maece/website/computer.html

Return to top.

# Editorial Requirements

Since many of the terms related to technology are spelled in a multiplicity of ways and are not yet offered in many dictionaries and spell-check programs, here is a list of potentially questionable words. Please spell them as they are written on this list. In particular, make note of words that are capitalized.

    e-mail
    FAQ
    home page
    HTML
    HTTP
    Internet
    intranet
    Listserv
    TELNET
    World Wide Web

Web
Web page
Web site
WWW

*Proof reading:*

All Web pages must be proof read by someone other than the original author in order to minimize typographical, grammatical and stylistic errors.

Return to top.

# Miscellaneous Requirements

Files should be named in lower case with the .html extension (for the sake of consistency .htm will no longer be accepted).

Graphics will all be kept in an <u>images</u> folder under the library folder on the WTAMU WWW server (example of a graphical link <img src="http://www.wtamu.edu/library/images/wtwton.gif" alt="WTAMU Homepage" align="left" width="108" height="36">). Please note that for the convenience of Web authors an image gallery is located on the P drive. You may also use images of your own choosing, provided they are accepted by the Webmaster. If you wish to use a new graphic, please provide source and copyright information to the Webmaster. In cases where the creator of a graphic has requested inclusion of source information on pages where the graphic is used, be sure to comply with this request.

Since all graphics will be held in a common folder on the Web site, make sure you check the folder (you can access the folder at the P drive) before naming images. This will avoid duplicate file names. If you have something with a very generic name (blue.gif), you should distinguish the image name by indicating the first few letters of your unit before the gif title. Example: govblue.gif

Return to top.

# Creativity

Despite our requirements, there is room for creating a site that reflects both the personality of your unit, and your Web design tastes. Bear in mind that the graphics, bullets, fonts, linking styles, layout, and language you choose will determine the look and feel as well as the tone of your Web pages.

Return to top.

# Subject Web Guides

In order to establish consistency in the presentation of Web guides, the general guidelines for Web page design are not sufficient. In addition to the guidelines for the Web site overall, a standard citation format will need to be used. Please observe the citation style below (including placement of italics, underline and so forth) for links to Web sites:

> *Britannica On-line* (WTAMU-affiliated only)
> http://www.eb.com:180
> An electronic version of the Encylopaedia Britannica, including articles not found in the print Britannica, Merriam-Webster's Collegiate Dictionary (Tenth Edition), the Britannica Book of the Year, and thousands of links to other World Wide Web sites. Searchable.

Print citations should emulate the style used in the discipline associated with the subject matter of the guide. For example, guides to literature should use MLA citation style, guides to Fine Arts should use APA style, and so forth. There is a notebook behind the Reference desk indicating the style used for each academic discipline.

A template for subject Web guides is located on the P drive, in a subject Web guides sub-folder in the Web Templates folder.

Return to top.

# Library Unit Pages

Library unit pages must include an FAQ. Site authors may use their own discretion in deciding whether the FAQ should exist as a single file, or as a series of smaller files. Authors should consider the length of the FAQ when making this decision. A relatively short FAQ may be rendered as one file, while a long FAQ will need to be broken into many short files (to save users from downloading a large file). Additionally, you may wish to choose a compromise between long files and short files, by breaking your FAQ up into groups of questions. Think about the nature of your particular FAQ, and weigh the options before designing the page. Don't forget to factor ease of printing into your decision.

Return to top.

# A Word About the Webmaster

- Please note that all pages (except personal Web pages) must be shown to the Webmaster before mounting them on the Web site.
- The Webmaster will not make any changes to pages except with the consent of the author of the pages in question. However, the Webmaster will make minor modifications to pages in cases where these modifications are related to site maintenance.
- Please note that the Webmaster reserves the right to remove pages that are outdated.
- You are free to contact the site Webmaster (Morven Fraser, x2211) and

discuss any one of the guidelines discussed above should you feel that they are not appropriate to your situation. Exceptions can be made.

Return to top.

# The Web Task Force

These guidelines were established by the Web Task Force in the summer of 1998. The task force is made up of Phillip Flores, Morven Fraser, Barbara Hightower, Shawna Kennedy-Witthar, Bennett Ponsford and Gonda Stayton. These guidelines were written with the aim of redeveloping the Web site for the fall of 1998.

Return to top.

**Hey, you aren't finished yet, you still need to see our design advice pages.**

---

*Authored by Morven Fraser, Reference/Distance Education Librarian.*
*E-mail: mfraser@mail.wtamu.edu*
*Comments to the Web Task Force.*
*All Contents copyright (c) 1998, WTAMU. All rights reserved.*
*Last revised: January 06, 1999.*
*http://www.wtamu.edu/library/html/guidelines.html*

**Western Carolina University**

**Hunter Library**
**Web Policy & Guidelines**

## Purpose:

Hunter Library's web site will support Hunter Library's mission by providing access to web- based research, instruction, and information.

The designated Webmaster will work with members of the Web Advisory Committee (WAC), all library units, and appropriate university agencies to keep the web site current and useful. WAC is made up of the Webmaster and representatives from Public Services and Technical Services, with the chair being the Head of Public Services.

## Content:

Each unit will have at least one page which will include the hours the unit is accessible, a link to the staff page listing unit personnel, and a brief description of the function or duties of the unit. Additional content, in support of each unit's mission, may be added as determined by the unit. Links to other sites will be selected using the same criteria for selecting other library material.

At a minimum, each Unit's home (index) page will include the following:

- Name of the library Unit.
- The appropriate telephone number.
- Date it was last updated, with the updater's initials or name. Make sure each time the page is updated that the date is also changed.
- Link back to the Library's Home Page.

Each subset of pages will provide a contact name and e-mail link for the person responsible for the page(s). Otherwise the Webmaster's name and e-mail link will be provided.

## Style:

It is important for the web site to have a consistent design format, so that users can easily identify when they are on library-created pages. Some unit's sub-pages may choose to follow a different style; if so, the style should complement the other pages and be applied consistently.

It is also expected that library web pages will:

- use a font style, size, and color that is clear and legible
- be grammatically correct and contain no misspelled words
- include few, if any, terms or phrases that would be considered "library jargon."

### Adding New Pages:

Library staff may create web pages for their unit and store them on the Library's LAN (Wcunw2) in the directory *H:\library\hompage\newstuff* .New web pages must first be reviewed by pertinent unit members and the unit head. Requests for these pages to be added to the web site will be directed to the WAC, who will review them within the context of the entire web site, and for compliance with the Web Policy.

The Webmaster will have the responsibility for transferring approved pages from Wcunw2 to the Library's site on the University Web server and will also be available to assist in making needed changes to existing Unit pages.

Remember that adding very large or complex files (text or graphics) will result in an inordinate drain on resources (e.g.: require heavy processing or generate high traffic). Justification for including large files must be provided to WAC.

Once a page has been linked to the Library's site, the URL (i.e.: filename and directory) will not be changed unless absolutely necessary.

### Changing/Maintaining Existing Pages:

Unit web pages will be maintained by the responsible unit. This responsibility includes simple updates and date changes, checking links periodically, keeping them up-to-date, and verifying that they contain information appropriate to the Library's mission.

Once you have made changes to your page, notify the webmaster so the revised page(s) can be uploaded.

Changes in library policies, staff, hours and services will be forwarded to the Webmaster for posting on the web site. These posted policies, hours and services should be reviewed by appropriate Unit Heads at the beginning of each semester to verify accuracy. Communications and Personnel Services will contact the Webmaster whenever there is a personnel change.

Substantial changes involving content or style will follow the same process as "adding new pages."

Restrictions: Personal home pages will not be linked to the Library's web pages. Resumes, etc, will be housed on the Vax only.

### The Standard Restrictions Apply:

Copyrighted materials will not be distributed or linked without the permission of the authors. More information about copyright can be found at http://lilibweb.sonoma.edu/Resources/copyright/, including information about "Copyright Considerations for Your Web Page."
[http://scilib.ucsd.edu/electclass/CopyrightTips.html]
*[compare with: http://www.lib.ncsu.edu/issues/SCC/copyright.html at NC State]*

The Western Carolina University Policy on the Use of Computers and Data Communication prohibits for-profit activity. Users and contributors to the Library's Web site are also bound by this policy. See http://www.wcu.edu/policy_cu.html .

Links will not be made to sites that contain questionable or illegal materials. For example: sites distributing illegal software, archives containing pornography, bulletin boards with defamatory, abusive or harassing materials.

The Web Advisory Committee and the University Librarian reserve the right to remove pages that do not conform to the Hunter Library Mission and the Web Policy.

**Internal Unit Pages:**
Documents used for library business will not be on the public web pages. Such documents can be linked to an internal web site for easy access to useful documents for library faculty and staff in pursuit of their professional duties. These documents might include policies, procedures, links to sites that provide unit-specific information, conference information, etc. The URL for this site is currently: http://www.wcu.edu/library/about/internal/index.htm. Units have the responsibility for the content of these pages. The Webmaster will transfer these files to the University Web Server.

The following copyright statement may be used when appropriate:
Copyright © [date], Western Carolina University. All rights reserved.
Approved by Hunter Council, mm/dd/yy

wbpolicy99.doc 2/99

| Humboldt | Library | Site Search | Catalyst | Subject Guides | Databases |

# Backpage - Web Design

## Introduction

- Overview
- Print Version of this Document

## Page Design

- Design Guidelines
- Standard Template
    - Header
    - Footer
    - Color palette
    - HTML standard

## Visual Elements

- Buttons, Icons, Bars, and Logos
- Graphics Guidelines
- Check your Page in other Browsers

## Loading Your Page

- Step-by-step Instructions
- Log in Screen

## Resources for Web Design

## Responsibilities

- Table of Responsibilities for Library Web Pages
- Web Committee
    - Members
    - Charge

Humboldt State University | Library | Site Search | Catalyst | Subject Guides | Databases
**The Library, Humboldt State University, One Harpst St., Arcata, California 95521-8299**
**Telephone: 707- 826-3441   Fax: 707- 826-3440**

**Policy Manual - 57**

Send comments and suggestions about this page to:
<u>infoservices@library.humboldt.edu</u>
Last Updated: December 22, 1997

| Humboldt | Library | Site Search | Catalyst | Subject Guides | Databases |

# Overview of Web Development

**Mission Statement**

The mission of the Humboldt State University Library Homepage is to provide a uniform electronic interface to identify information resources available in and through the Library, in whatever format they currently reside, and to provide access to those resources available electronically.

**Policies**

**Procedures**

Humboldt State University | Library | Site Search | Catalyst | Subject Guides | Databases
**The Library, Humboldt State University, One Harpst St., Arcata, California 95521-8299**
**Telephone: 707- 826-3441   Fax: 707- 826-3440**

Send comments and suggestions about this page to:
infoservices@library.humboldt.edu
Last Updated: March 10, 1997

| Humboldt | Library | Site Search | Catalyst | Subject Guides | Databases |

# Design Guidelines

The goal of web design for the HSU Library homepage is to provide information in a visually pleasing manner with a minimum of distractions. To reach the largest population, pages are designed to be optimally viewable on Netscape browsers version 2.01 and above. Pages are to be designed for a screen 640 pixels wide by 480 pixels high. Graphics should be designed at 72 dots per inch and in 8-bit 256 colors. The design dicta below reflect this philosophy.

- No blinking images
- If frames are used, a non-frame alternative must be offered and maintained
- No Java applets
- Do not use "under construction" signs

Humboldt State University | Library | Site Search | Catalyst | Subject Guides | Databases
**The Library, Humboldt State University, One Harpst St., Arcata, California 95521-8299**
**Telephone: 707- 826-3441   Fax: 707- 826-3440**

Send comments and suggestions about this page to:
infoservices@library.humboldt.edu
Last Updated: March 31, 1997

| Humboldt | Library | Site Search | Catalyst | Subject Guides | Databases |

# Standard Template for HSU Library Web Pages

## Guidelines

- Design target specifications: to reach the largest population with the Library's web page, all graphics should be designed at 72 dots per inch and in 8-bit 256 colors for a screen 640 pixels wide by 480 pixels high
- **Page size** should be limited to the size of most browser screens (640x480 pixels)
- "Top pages" should contain few items and lots of space
- All pages shall comply with the WC3 HTML 3.2 standard (no proprietary tags)
- **Background color** of all pages shall be white <body bgcolor="#ffffff">
- Other colors shall be chosen from the nondithering palette
- **Times Roman Font** shall be used in all Library web pages
- **Standard header** shall contain the HSU Library logo, and <H1> heading for HSU Library and <H2> heading that reflects the textual page title
- **Standard footer** shall contain:
  - standard Library buttons
  - text version of standard buttons
  - a "last updated" statement
  - an email link to the responsible party
  - appropriate "return to" buttons
    - return to top of page/table of contents
    - return to previous level
    - return to Library homepage
- **Table of contents** - if pages are more than 4 screens in length, place a hyperlinked table of contents at the top of the page
- **Accuracy and spelling** should be carefully checked before loading pages

Humboldt State University | Library | Site Search | Catalyst | Subject Guides | Databases
**The Library, Humboldt State University, One Harpst St., Arcata, California 95521-8299**
**Telephone: 707- 826-3441 Fax: 707- 826-3440**

Send comments and suggestions about this page to:
infoservices@library.humboldt.edu
Last Updated: March 28, 1997

| Humboldt | Library | Site Search | Catalyst | Subject Guides | Databases |

# HSU Library Header & Footer Templates

Copy these directly into a word processing file, then edit according to instructions. Hint: keep blank templates on your own hard drive or disk after you've deleted the instructions within the square brackets.

## Header Template

```
&ltHTML>
&ltHEAD>
<!--Comment lines to aid in document administration?-->
<!
Author:          [insert your name here]
Department:      [insert the name of responsible unit he
Creation Date:   [insert original date here]
Revision Hist:   [insert latest revised date here]
File Name:       [insert file name here]
Image Files:     [list all image files here]
Description:     [describe the purpose of the file here]
-->
&ltTITLE>[insert your title here]</TITLE>
</HEAD>
&ltBODY BGCOLOR="#FFFFFF">
&ltIMG SRC=[insert chosen logo here]>
&ltP>
&ltH2>[insert your title here]</H2>
&ltimg src="../../red.gif" width="100%" height="5"
alt="-------------------------------------------------
&ltP>
```

## Footer Template:

```
&ltP>
&ltimg src="../../red.gif" width="100%" height="5"
alt="-------------------------------------------------
&ltP>
&ltCENTER>&ltA HREF="lbuttons.html">[insert chosen butt
here]</A></CENTER>&ltBR>
&ltCENTER>[insert text version of buttons here]</CENTER
&ltP>
Send comments and suggestions about this page to &ltA
```

```
HREF="mailto[responsible party's email address]"&gtresp
party</A>&ltBR> Last updated: [month day, year]&ltBR>
&ltP>
[appropriate "return to" buttons: top of page/table of
level, Library homepage]
</BODY>
</HTML>
```

Humboldt State University | Library | Site Search | Catalyst | Subject Guides | Databases
**The Library, Humboldt State University, One Harpst St., Arcata, California 95521-8299**
**Telephone: 707- 826-3441   Fax: 707- 826-3440**

Send comments and suggestions about this page to:
infoservices@library.humboldt.edu
Last updated: March 19, 1997

| Humboldt | Library | Site Search | Catalyst | Subject Guides | Databases |

# Color Palette

- <u>216 Safe Colors for Browsers</u> (Nondithering Colors by Hue)
- <u>ASCII-to-hex color conversion (for use in HTML Code)</u>
- <u>Mediarama's Hex Converter</u>

Send comments and suggestions about this page to:
<u>infoservices@library.humboldt.edu</u>
Last Updated: March 6, 1997

| Humboldt | Library | Site Search | Catalyst | Subject Guides | Databases |

# HTML Standard

- Kinder, Gentler HTML Validator
- HTML 3.2 Specifications
  - Introducing HTML 3.2
  - see especially HTML Reference Specifications
  - and The Structure of HTML 3.2 Documents

Send comments and suggestions about this page to:
infoservices@library.humboldt.edu
Last Updated: March 6, 1997

| Humboldt | Library | Site Search | Catalyst | Subject Guides | Databases |

# Buttons, Icons, and Logos

- Library buttons
- Library logos
- Button and Icon Factory
- Realm Graphics
- Indexes of Icons and Graphics
- Clip Art Connection
- Transparent/Interlaced GIF Resource Page
- Icons, Flags, Symbols
- FAQ on Making Transparent and Interlaced GIFs
- Chris Stephens' Buttons, Bullets, Bars

Humboldt State University | Library | Site Search | Catalyst | Subject Guides | Databases
**The Library, Humboldt State University, One Harpst St., Arcata, California  95521-8299**
**Telephone:  707- 826-3441   Fax:  707- 826-3440**

Send comments and suggestions about this page to:
infoservices@library.humboldt.edu
Last Updated: March 6, 1997

# Graphics Guidelines

- Use interlaced GIF images for all graphic files above 80k
- Predefine the height and width of images in your HTML file
- Use the Alt attribute of the IMG tag for those who choose not to load images and for non-graphical browsers
- Use transparent backgrounds
- Use small images (thumbnails) linked to larger versions whenever possible to quicken download time
- Provide a text-only alternate page when appropriate

Send comments and suggestions about this page to:
infoservices@library.humboldt.edu
Last Updated: March 28, 1997

| Humboldt | Library | Site Search | Catalyst | Subject Guides | Databases |

# Check your Page in other Browsers

- Bobby
- lynx-me

Humboldt State University | Library | Site Search | Catalyst | Subject Guides | Databases
**The Library, Humboldt State University, One Harpst St., Arcata, California 95521-8299**
**Telephone: 707- 826-3441    Fax: 707- 826-3440**

Send comments and suggestions about this page to:
infoservices@library.humboldt.edu
Last Updated: March 6, 1997

| Humboldt | Library | Site Search | Catalyst | Subject Guides | Databases |

# Resources for Web Design

## Comprehensive Pages

- Lynda's Homegurrl's Links O'Interest
- University of Iowa Libraries Web Builders and Multimedia Resources
- Digital Frontiers Web Graphics Development Resources
- Network Communications Design Homepage
  - US NCD Mirror Site

## Color

- 216 Safe Colors for Browsers (Nondithering Colors by Hue)
- ASCII-to-hex Color Conversion (for use in HTML Code
- Mediarama's Hex Converter

## Images

- Complete Resource for All Web Builders
- Button and Icon Factory
- Realm Graphics
- Indexes of Icons and Graphics
- Clip Art Connection
- Transparent/Interlaced GIF Resource Page
- Icons, Flags, Symbols
- FAQ on Making Transparent and Interlaced GIFs
- Chris Stephens' Buttons, Bullets, Bars
- DIP Guide to Digital Pictures
- GIF Wizard

## HTML

- Kinder, Gentler, HTML Validator
- HTML 3.2 Specifications
  - Introducing HTML 3.2
  - see especially HTML Reference Specifications
  - and The Structure of HTML 32. Documents

## Type

- Type Faces that Work Together (Daniel Will-Harris)

## Browsers and Monitors

- Bobby

- lynx-me
- Monitor Gamma (Robert Berger)

---

Humboldt State University | Library | Site Search | Catalyst | Subject Guides | Databases
**The Library, Humboldt State University, One Harpst St., Arcata, California  95521-8299**
**Telephone:  707- 826-3441   Fax:  707- 826-3440**

---

Send comments and suggestions about this page to:
infoservices@library.humboldt.edu
Last Updated: October 29, 1997

| Humboldt | Library | Site Search | Catalyst | Subject Guides | Databases |

# Library Web Development Committee

1. **Name**: Library Web Development Committee -- Standing
2. **Function**: To design and continue development of the Library's webpage(s), building upon the Library's present guidelines and within University policies and guides for such development.
3. **Responsibilities**:
   1. The committee will bear responsibility for maintaining and developing the Library's style guide, including the "Backpage."
   2. The committee is not reponsible for maintenance or technical aspects of the work associated with a webpage.
4. **Membership**:
   1. One representative from Access Services
   2. One representative from Information Services
   3. Two representatives appointed at large
   4. One representative from Systems
   5. One student-employee representative
5. **Terms of membership**: Members are appointed for 2-year staggered terms by the University Librarian.
6. **Chair**: Chair to be appointed annually from among the members of the committee by the University Librarian.
7. **Reporting**:
   1. Recommendations are forwarded to the Library Council and University Librarian.
   2. Agenda and minutes to be made available to the Library staff by appropriate means.

Reviewed by Library Council, 8/19/97

---

Humboldt State University | Library | Site Search | Catalyst | Subject Guides | Databases
**The Library, Humboldt State University, One Harpst St., Arcata, California 95521-8299**
**Telephone: 707- 826-3441 Fax: 707- 826-3440**

Send comments and suggestions about this page to: Information Services
Last Updated: December 22, 1997

## OWENS LIBRARY

# WEB PUBLISHING STANDARDS

**Owens Library Web publishing standards:**

- Promote consistency in design and content of Owens Library Web pages
- Ensure first and second level pages incorporate essential elements of the proposed University Web publishing standards
- Encourage development of third level pages (pages three clicks from the university home page)and underpages (pages four clicks or more from the university home page) that are engaging and functional
- Provide content guidelines which address the specifics of compiling and maintaining bibliographies, research guides, tutorials, and webliographies
- Outline the implentation process for Owens Library Web pages
- Direct Web page authors and editors to appropriate resources through the **Resources for Web Authors** page

---

About Owens Library Web Pages
Created (August 1998)
Revised (January 1999)
Author: Frank Baudino
© Copyrighted Material

| Owens Library | Northwest Missouri State University |

**NORTHWEST MISSOURI STATE UNIVERSITY**

**OWENS LIBRARY**

# WEB PAGE ADDITIONS AND WITHDRAWALS

Additions & Withdrawals

Annotation Writing

Content Guidelines

Copyright

Files & Folders

Implementation Process

Resources for Web Authors

Selection

- Templates
- Second Level
- Third Level & Underpages

Web Page Maintenance Schedule

Web Partners

Title of Page [                    ]

URL of Page: http://www.nwmissouri.edu/library/
[                    ]

Date Page Created (mm/yyyy)
[                    ]
(or loaded onto the server)

Author of Page Content [                    ]

Code Editor [                    ]

Content Editor [                    ]

Basic Editor [                    ]

Date Page Withdrawn from Server (mm/dd/yyyy)
[                    ]

Return to the Web Publishing Standards page.

URL for this page: http://www.nwmissouri.edu/library/owens/guidelines/webpage.htm

About Owens Library Web Pages
Created (July 1998)
Revised (January 2000)
Author: Joyce A. Meldrem
© Copyrighted Material

| Owens Library | Northwest Missouri State University |

**OWENS LIBRARY**

# CONTENT GUIDELINES: ANNOTATION WRITING

| **Examples** | **Vocabulary** |

**Annotations are used to describe entries in bibliographies and webliographies. Annotations should:**

- Be written in full sentences
- Describe the important features of the Web page or Web site succinctly
- Use keywords which facilitate using Internet search tools (The patron should be able to use the browser's **Find** command to locate a particular entry on the Web page containing certain keywords or find a particular Web page by entering keywords in the Search These Pages search engine. Further explanation is provided in Examples below.)
- Provide a link to the authority responsible for page content in the case of annotations for Internet links on a webliography page
- Place the following centered disclaimer just above the "*return to course/subject resources*" statement on all bibliographies and webliographies that include quoted materials: **All quoted material is from the respective source.**
- Employ recommended vocabulary standards

**EXAMPLES:**

**The first example is taken from the HPERD Sources in Owens Library page.**

*Encyclopedia of Nutrition and Good Health* 613.203 R77e 3RD FLOOR
This encyclopedia provides current information on foods, food technology, food labels, vitamins, minerals, and major nutrients. In addition, there are discussions of food related conditions such as eating disorders, obesity, addiction, dieting and weight loss, food sensitivities and chronic degenerative diseases.

The keywords in this entry facilitate using Internet search tools. If a patron used the browser's **Find** command to search through entries in the **HPERD WWW Resources** page with the words weight loss, they would locate this entry. Or if the patron used the **Search These Pages** search engine, the page containing this entry would appear in the result list.

This annotation is written in full sentences.

**The second example is taken from the HPERD WWW Resources page.**

Internet Public Library: Health & Medical Sciences Ready Reference
This page contains links to resources covering such topics as alcohol/drugs/tobacco, anatomy, disabilities, diseases/disorders/syndromes, exercise and fitness and many other

*Return to the top of the page*

**VOCABULARY:** Particular words and phrases are repeated throughout the Owens Library Web pages. If the words or phrases that follow are included in annotations or anywhere on a library Web page, use them as they appear below:

| | |
|---|---|
| Owens Library catalog | InfoTrac |
| library catalog | EBSCOhost |
| online | MasterFILE FullTEXT 1000 |
| homepage | E-mail |
| Web site | Internet |
| full-text | Web |

*Return to the top of the page*

Return to the <u>Web Publishing Standards</u> page.

URL for this page: http://www.nwmissouri.edu/library/owens/guidelines/annotation.htm

About Owens Library Web Pages
Created (August 1998)
Revised (November 1999)
Author: Frank Baudino
© Copyrighted Material

| <u>Owens Library</u> | <u>Northwest Missouri State University</u> |

**OWENS LIBRARY**

# CONTENT GUIDELINES

Additions & Withdrawals

Annotation Writing

Content Guidelines

Copyright

Files & Folders

Implementation Process

Resources for Web Authors

Selection

Templates
- Second Level
- Third Level & Underpages

Web Page Maintenance Schedule

Web Partners

**Content guidelines will assist Owens Library Web page authors and content editors in compiling and maintaining bibliographies, research guides, tutorials and webliographies.**

*Specifically, the content guidelines:*

- Promote selection of Web pages for bibliographies and webliographies which are substantial and authoritative
- Provide examples on how to write annotations which are clear, descriptive, and facilitate using Internet search tools
- Establish vocabulary standards for terms and phrases used frequently in library Web pages
- Ensure copyright compliance on all library Web pages

Return to the Web Publishing Standards page.

URL for this page: http://www.nwmissouri.edu/library/owens/guidelines/content.htm

About Owens Library Web Pages
Created (August 1998)
Revised (November 1999)
Author: Frank Baudino
© Copyrighted Material

| Owens Library | Northwest Missouri State University |

**NORTHWEST MISSOURI STATE UNIVERSITY**

## OWENS LIBRARY

# CONTENT GUIDELINES: COPYRIGHT

| Types | Exemptions | Limitations | Recommended Limits |

1. **Types of work that may be covered under copyright include:**
   - motion media
   - text material
   - lyrics, music, music videos
   - illustrations and photographs
   - numerical data sets
2. **Works exempted from copyright restrictions include:**
   - United States government works
   - works on which the copyright has expired (Link to the When Works Pass into the Public Domain chart for a list of works that fall into the public domain.)
   - works on the Web which grant permission for use under certain conditions (such as proper attribution and a back link to the page of origin)
3. **Three limitations on Fair Use are:**
   - time
   - portion
   - copying and distribution
4. **Recommended limits for multimedia works:**
   - 10% or 3 minutes, whichever is less, in the aggregate of a copyrighted motion media work may be reproduced or otherwise incorporated
   - 10% or 1000 words, whichever is less, in the aggregate of a copyrighted work consisting of text material may be reproduced or otherwise incorporated
   - 10%, but in no event more than 30 seconds, of the music and lyrics from an individual musical work may be reproduced or otherwise incorporated
   - no more than 5 images by an artist or photographer may be reproduced or otherwise incorporated
   - not more than 10% or 15 images, whichever is less, may be reproduced or otherwise incorporated from photographs and illustrations in a published collective work
   - 10% or 2500 fields or cell entries, whichever is less, from a copyrighted database or data table may be reproduced or otherwise incorporated

*Return to the top of the page*

This page is adapted with permission from the **Fair Use Guidelines For Educational Multimedia** page in the Limitations section. For further information on copyright issues and fair use as it applies to the Internet, consult Carolyn Johnson's Copyright Resources page.

Return to the Web Publishing Standards page.

URL for this page: http://www.nwmissouri.edu/library/owens/guidelines/copyright.htm

**Northwest Missouri State University**

| Owens Library | Northwest Missouri State University |

OWENS LIBRARY

# FILES AND FOLDERS
| Folders | Files | Graphics Files |

**These are guidelines pertaining to WWW files and folders on the library WSG/A+ Library Homepage folder or on the university server:**

## Folders

- The only folders under the **WSG/A+ Library Homepage** folder or in the library m500001 top level directory should correspond to the 2nd level pages on the library front page.
- This same pattern should be reflected in front pages at other levels. For instance the only folders under the **Course/Subject** folder should correspond to the main headings or categories represented on the **Course/Subject** front page.
- Do not create a directory in the m500001 account on the university server that is more that four levels deep. (For instance, creating an **Education** directory under the **Course/Subject** directory would be three levels deep. Creating a **Secondary Education** directory under the **Education** directory would be four levels deep. Creating a directory under **Secondary Education** would be five levels deep and would not be functional.)

# Files

- Work from files in the **WSG/A+ Library Home Page** folder on the library server.
- Use the **Save As...** command to create a copy of any file to be edited, renaming the copy to another filename such as **Filename1.htm**.
- Work from the copy until final revisions are made and the page is ready to FTP to the university server.
- When revisions are complete, **Rename** the original file to **Filenameold.htm** (or some other appropriate and obvious filename). Then rename the copy from **Filename1.htm** (or whatever filename you used while revising it) to the original **Filename.htm**.
- Be extremely careful when revising or FTPing files that are named **index.htm** or **index.html**. If you copy or move with FTP a file named **index.htm** or **index.html** into the wrong folder or directory you will cause confusion and possibly overwrite files or destroy data.

# Graphics Files

- Graphics files common to most pages should be included in the **Images** folder and pages addressing these image files should have a relative link to them in the **img** tag (eg. **<img src="../images/level2.gif">** ).
- Graphics files which are common to a small group of interrelated pages should be placed in the folder or directory containing those related files. For instance, graphics files common to only psychology pages should be placed in the Psychology folder or sub-directory. The relative link for these graphics files should be **<img src="filename.gif">**.
- To avoid confusion, graphics file names should be appropriate and reflect the type of pages they are used in or the function they serve. For instance, a GIF file for the heading of the **Education Research Guide** could be named **edresearchheader.gif**. It should not be named something generic such as **25.gif** or **header.gif**.

Return to Web Publishing Standards Page

URL for this page: http://www.nwmissouri.edu/library/owens/guidelines/file.htm

About Owens Library Web Pages
Created (October 1998)
Revised (November 1999)
Author: Frank Baudino
© Copyrighted Material

| Owens Library | Northwest Missouri State University |

**OWENS LIBRARY**

# IMPLEMENTATION PROCESS

1. This process applies to all pages that are new or significantly revised. The page author or code editor with FTP privileges will FTP the page to the library account on the VAX and link the new page to the appropriate place on the library Web site. The author will notify library personnel of the URL where the page can be viewed. The web page will be reviewed for consistency with the library standards and content guidelines.
2. A deadline date of 10 working days will be given by the author for library personnel to make suggestions for improving the page. Final decisions about suggestions made are the responsibility of the page author.
3. At the end of the 10 day time period:
   - **If no changes are made** the page will be considered approved.
   - **If changes to the page are made,** library personnel will be notified by the author and another time period of 2 days will be in effect so library personnel may view these changes. After this deadline the page will be considered completed and approved.
4. **When the page is considered approved,** the page author will fill out a *Owens Library Web Page Additions & Deletions* form. This form is linked from the Web Publishing Standards page.

Return to the Web Publishing Standards page.

URL for this page: http://www.nwmissouri.edu/library/owens/guidelines/approval.htm

About Owens Library Web Pages
Created (August 1998)
Revised (November 1999)
Author: Frank Baudino
© Copyrighted Material

| Owens Library | Northwest Missouri State University |

**NORTHWEST MISSOURI STATE UNIVERSITY**

**OWENS LIBRARY**

Additions & Withdrawals

Annotation Writing

Content Guidelines

Copyright

Files & Folders

Implementation Process

Resources for Web
Authors

Selection

> Templates
> - Second Level
> - Third Level &
>   Underpages

Web Page Maintenance
Schedule

Web Partners

# RESOURCES FOR WEB AUTHORS

## HTML and Javascript

- **Beginner's Guide to HTML**
- **CNET Builder.com**
- **Composing Good HTML**
- **HTML Resources**
- **Web Developer's Virtual Library**
- **Webmonkey**

## Other Resources

- **Copyright Clearance Center**
- **Copyright Resources**
- **Dictionaries, Thesauri and Acronyms**
- **Validation Tools**
- **Web Page Design Resources**

Return to the Web Publishing Standards page.

URL for this page: http://www.nwmissouri.edu/library/owens/guidelines/resources.htm

| Owens Library | Northwest Missouri State University |

## OWENS LIBRARY

### CONTENT GUIDELINES: SELECTION

**Selection guidelines assist Owens Library Web page authors and content editors in compiling and maintaining webliographies.**

*When selecting Web pages, keep in mind these criteria:*

- Authority (Who is the author/sponsor of the page? What are the author's credentials?)
- Design (Is the page easy to use? Does the organization of material support the page's purpose?)
- Accuracy (Where does the information come from? Has the information been peer reviewed or refereed?)
- Purpose (Is the page informational, educational, political, recreational, commercial or a combination of one or more of these?)
- Target (Who is the intended audience of the page?)

For further explanation of these criteria with representative examples of each type, link to the Evaluating Web Sites page.

Return to the Web Publishing Standards page.

URL for this page: http://www.nwmissouri.edu/library/owens/guidelines/selection.html

---

About Owens Library Web Pages
Created (August 1998)
Revised (November 1999)
Author: Frank Baudino
© Copyrighted Material

| Owens Library | Northwest Missouri State University |

Northwest Missouri State University

OWENS LIBRARY

# TEMPLATES

| Exceptions | Second Level | Third Level & Underpages |

Templates are guides for designing Owens Library Web pages. To use a template, load the template file into an HTML editor and use the **Save As** command to save the file to the desired location with a new file name. Then modify the configuration and text as needed. Adherence to these standards begins with new pages or when old pages are revised.

- Second level pages should include the standard header and footer.
- Third level pages (pages three clicks from the university home page) and underpages (pages four clicks or more from the university home page) may include the standard header, but must incorporate the standard footer.
- Third level pages and underpages which constitute exceptions should have a consistent design and presentation of content, especially if they are small groups of pages closely interrelated by function or subject.
- Graphics should provide useful visual clues about the information provided on the page. Graphics should load quickly. Use the ALT command in your source code to indicate text to be displayed if graphics do not load.
- Graphics files common to most pages should be included in the images folder and pages addressing these image files should have a relative link to them in the img tag (eg. **<img src="../images/level2.gif">** ).
- Graphics files which are common to a small group of interrelated pages should be placed in the folder or directory containing those related files. For instance, graphics files common to only psychology pages should be placed in the Psychology folder or directory.
- New or significantly revised library Web pages must go through the Implementation Process.
- **Exceptions:**
  - Interactive learning web pages (i.e., Freshman Seminar, English Composition, Using Computers, Library Success Guide, webliographies, research guides and tutorials) may have a distinctive look which encourages student interaction.
  - A set of related pages pertaining to a common subject, department or course should have a consistent design. If backgrounds and different colored fonts are used they should be subdued in character and design.
  - Team Web pages may use designs and formats which reflect the character of the team. The look and appearance of these pages will be approved by the appropriate team prior to being linked to the Owens Library Web Page. These pages must still go through the Implementation Process if new or significantly revised.

Return to Web Publishing Standards Page

URL for this page: http://www.nwmissouri.edu/library/owens/guidelines/template.htm

| Owens Library | Northwest Missouri State University |

**NORTHWEST MISSOURI STATE UNIVERSITY**

**OWENS LIBRARY**

# TEMPLATES: SECOND LEVEL, NO COMMENTS

**NOTE:** To use a version of the second level template with comments, click here.

To use this template, load this file into an HTML editor and use the **Save As** command to save the file to the desired location with a new file name. Then modify the configuration and text as needed. Second level pages adhere to these guidelines when newly created or revised:

- Use the standard header and footer (include Code Editor or Editor only if they are a different person from the page Author)
- Use consistent font style and font size in the main body of the page
- New or significantly revised library Web pages must go through the Implementation Process
- Using the three cell format present on the main body of this template is strictly optional
- Using the 560 pixel width format for the main body of the page is strictly optional

Return to the Web Publishing Standards page.

URL for this page: http://www.nwmissouri.edu/library/owens/guidelines/tempsecond.htm

About Owens Library Web Pages
Created (October 1998)
Revised (November 1999)
Author: Frank Baudino
Code Editor:
Editor:
© Copyrighted Material
Put back link credits here.

| Owens Library | Northwest Missouri State University |

NORTHWEST MISSOURI STATE UNIVERSITY

**OWENS LIBRARY**

NORTHWEST MISSOURI STATE UNIVERSITY

**OWENS LIBRARY**

# TEMPLATE: THIRD LEVEL & UNDERPAGES, NO COMMENTS

**NOTE:** To view a template with comments, click here.

To use this template, load this file into an HTML editor and use the **Save As** command to save the file to the desired location with a new file name. Then modify the configuration and text as needed. Adherence to these guidelines begin when new pages are added or pages are revised:

- Use the standard footer (include Code Editor or Editor only if they are a different person from the page Author).
- Use consistent font style and font size in the main body of the page
- Using a standard header is optional (especially if the pages being created fall under the exceptions)
- Using the three cell format for the main body of the page is optional
- Using a 560 pixel width for main body of the page is optional
- Place the following centered disclaimer just above the "*Return to .... page.*" statement on all bibliographies and webliographies that include quoted materials: **All quoted material is from the respective source.**

Return to the Web Publishing Standards page.

URL for this page: http://www.nwmissouri.edu/library/owens/guidelines/tempthird.htm

| Owens Library | Northwest Missouri State University |

OWENS LIBRARY

# WEB PARTNERS

| Types of Involvement | Forming Partnerships | Training Options |

The Web Partners initiative encourages voluntary participation in Web page publication. The types of participation outlined below are correspond to roles currently played by library personnel in their relationship to the way the library functions - the roles of processing of materials and providing authority control. New roles and relationships can be established between Web partners as individuals develop new skills and insight and as the nature of library services changes over time.

Types of involvement are outlined first followed by the process for selecting types of involvement, accessing appropriate training, forming partnerships, and adjusting the Web page maintenance schedule. This process also includes setting priorities for creating new pages and significantly redesigning existing pages.

Finally, the kinds of training library personnel can receive are indicated and who will be responsible for coordinating this training. Web content guidelines include templates for common types of subject pages now produced such as bibliographies (Print Sources pages), research guides (How to conduct research pages) and webliographies (WWW Resources pages). These guidelines incorporate recommendations for writing annotations, selecting new links and assuring copyright compliance.

## Types of involvement:

A. **Editor** (Skills needed: familiarity with Windows 95, Web searching knowledge, familiarity with subject or discipline, familiarity with Web page design standards and content guidelines )

    a) Check for broken links
    b) Spell check and grammar check
    c) Check accuracy of annotations
    d) Checks for appropriateness of links or sources
    e) Adds links or sources

B. **Code Editor** (Skills needed: familiarity with Windows 95, knowledge of HTML coding and Web page editors, familiarity with Web page design standards and content guidelines, FTP knowledge)

C. **Author(s)** Compiler(s) of Web page content (Skills needed: knowledge of content guidelines and design standards, familiarity with subject or discipline, competence using a graphics capable browser and Microsoft Word)

*Return to the top of the page*

## Forming partnerships:

1. Choose a type(s) of involvement subject to the approval of your team.
2. Choose an author to partner with from the Web page editing schedule or consult with the Web Study Group about creating new pages.
3. Attend general group training sessions. Then arrange for individual consultations as needed.
4. Meet with partner that is assigned the subject area of the page(s) chosen according to Web page editing schedule.
5. Adjust editing schedule to meet the requirements of the page to be edited and the work flow of the partners.
6. Begin editing.
7. Communicate regularly with partner.
8. Select another type of involvement when interested, ready and workload permits subject to the approval of your team.

*Return to the top of the page*

## Training options:

1. Group training (Pat Danner and Carolyn Johnson will coordinate)
2. Individual consultation (Chuck Vaughn will coordinate)
3. Self-guided training (Pat McFarland and Connie Ury will coordinate)
4. Mixed training (a combination of two or more options listed above)

*Return to the top of the page*

Return to the Web Publishing Standards page.

URL for this page: http://www.nwmissouri.edu/library/owens/guidelines/partners.html

About Owens Library Web Pages
Created (August 1998)
Revised (November 1999)
Author: Frank Baudino
© Copyrighted Material

| Owens Library | Northwest Missouri State University |

# List of Owens Library Web Pages

## Update schedule

| | |
|---|---|
| Webliographies | Summer or by request |
| Bibliographies | Fall or by request |
| Research Guides | Spring or by request |
| Tutorials | As needed |
| About US | Summer |
| Front Page | As needed but at least once per year |
| 2nd Level Page | As needed but at least once per year |

| Title of Page | URL | Date Created | Content Author | HTML Code Editor | Content Editor | Basic Editor | Update schedule |
|---|---|---|---|---|---|---|---|
| **OWENS LIBRARY HOME PAGE** | http://www.nwmissouri.edu/library/ | | | | | | |
| Home Page | index.html | Summer 96 | Info Team | Joyce | | | |
| | about.htm | June-98 | Chuck | Chuck | Chuck | Chuck | |
| **SERVICES** | | | | | | | |
| **CITING THE INTERNET** | | | | | | | |
| Citing the Internet | citing/citing.htm | August-96 | Carolyn | Consultant | | | |
| **EMAIL A QUESTION** | | | | | | | |
| Email a question | question/index.htm | March-98 | Frank | Frank | | | |
| **FACULTY OFFICE CALLS** | | | | | | | |
| Faculty Office Calls | services/officecalls.htm | February-98 | Vicki/Carolyn | Consultant | | | |
| **INTERLIBRARY LOAN REQUESTS** | | | | | | | |
| Interlibrary Loan Online Forms | ill/index.htm | February-98 | Glenn | Consultant | | | |
| Book Request Form | ill/bookform.htm | February-98 | Glenn | Consultant | | | |
| Photocopy Request Form | ill/photocopy.htm | February-98 | Glenn | Consultant | | | |
| **LIBRARY HOURS** | | | | | | | |
| Library Hours | hours/hours.htm | Summer 96 | Vicki | Vicki | Vicki | Vicki | |
| **RESEARCH CONSULTATIONS** | | | | | | | |
| Student Research Consultation | services/paper.htm | Summer 96 | Joyce | Joyce | | | |
| **RESOURCES** | | | | | | | |
| **COURSE SUBJECT RESOURCES** | | | | | | | |
| Agriculture | | | | | | | |

| Resource | URL | February-98 | Frank/Karen | Frank/Consultant | |
|---|---|---|---|---|---|
| General Agriculture Resources | courses/agriculture/agriculture.htm | February-98 | Vicki | Vicki | |
| **Biography** | | | | | |
| Biography Sources | courses/biography/biosources.html | March-98 | Vicki | Vicki | |
| Biographical Research Guide | courses/biography/bioresearch.html | February-98 | Vicki | Vicki | |
| Biographical WWW Resources | courses/biography/biowww.html | February-98 | Vicki | Vicki | |
| **Business** | | | | | |
| Business Research Guide | courses/business/bsnsguide.htm | September-98 | Joyce | Joyce | |
| Business Sources | courses/business/business.htm | August-97 | Joyce | Consultant | |
| Business WWW Resources | courses/business/index.html | February-98 | Joyce | Consultant | |
| Researching a Company | courses/business/companyresearch.html | August-98 | Joyce | Consultant | |
| International Business WWW Resources | courses/business/international.html | February-98 | Joyce | Joyce | |
| World Information Sources in Owens | courses/business/world.htm | August-97 | Joyce | Karen | |
| Finding Articles About Management Information Systems Topics | courses/mis/articles2.html | January-99 | Connie | Connie | |
| MIS Tools WWW Resources | courses/mis/mistools.htm | March-99 | Connie | Connie | Connie |
| Management Information Systems Resources | mis/mis.htm | September-97 | Carolyn | Consultant | |
| Online Searchable Newspaper Sites | articles/newssites.htm | Fall-97 | Joyce | Joyce | |
| Statistics Sources | courses/business/statistics.htm | August-97 | Joyce | Joyce | |
| Statistics WWW Resources | courses/business/statisticswww.html | August-98 | Joyce | | |
| Checkpoint | www.checkpoint.riag.com/ | | Joyce | | |
| **Careers** | | | | | |
| Career Sources in Owens | courses/careers/owenscareers.htm | Summer 96 | Joyce | Joyce | |
| Careers WWW Resources | courses/careers/careers.htm | Summer 96 | Carolyn | | |
| **College Choice** | | | | | |
| College Choice and Financial Aid Sources | courses/finaid/college.htm | Summer 96 | Vicki | Vicki | |
| College Choice, Scholarships & financial Aid WWW Resources | courses/finaid/collegechoice.htm | February-98 | Vicki | Vicki | |
| **Computer Science/Information Systems** | | | | | |
| CS/IS Senior Seminar Research Guide | courses/computers/csis.html | January-99 | Carolyn | Carolyn | Carolyn |
| **Computers and Society** | | | | | |
| Computers and Society Research Guide | courses/computers/computerethicsresearch.ht | July-99 | Connie | Connie | |
| Computers and Society WWW Resources | courses/computers/computerethics.htm | July-99 | Connie | Connie | |
| **Copyright** | | | | | |

| Title | URL | Date | | | | |
|---|---|---|---|---|---|---|
| Copyright Resources | courses/copyright/resources.html | June-98 | Carolyn | Carolyn | Carolyn | Carolyn |
| **Drama** | | | | | | |
| Drama and Theatre Research Guide | courses/theatre/index.htm | April-98 | Frank | Frank | | |
| Drama and Theatre Sources | courses/theatre/theatresources.htm | April-98 | Frank | Frank | | |
| Drama and Theatre WWW Resources | courses/theatre/theatrewww.htm | April-98 | Frank | Frank | | |
| **Education** | | | | | | |
| Education Research Guide | courses/education/educationresearch.html | December-97 | Vicki/Connie | Vicki/Connie | | |
| Education Sources | courses/education2/educationsource.htm | May-99 | MEK/Frank | MEK/Frank | | |
| Education WWW Resources | courses/education2/education.htm | June-96 | Joyce | Joyce | | |
| Children's Literature Sources | courses/education2/childlitowens.htm | November-98 | MEK | MEK/Leigh | | |
| Children's Literature WWW Resources | courses/education2/children.htm | September-98 | Calfee | | | |
| Distance Education | courses/education2/distance.htm | September-98 | Carolyn/Joyce | Carolyn/Joyce | | |
| Elementary Mathematics WWW Resources | courses/education2/elementary.html | June-98 | Carolyn | Carolyn | | |
| Learning Disabilities WWW Resources | ccourses/education2/wwwld.html | October-98 | Connie/Joyce | Connie/Joyce | Connie/Joyce | Connie/Joyce |
| Identifying, Evaluating and Annotating Multicultural WWW Resources | courses/education2/multicultural.htm | January-99 | Connie | Connie | | |
| Multiculturalism in Education | education2/multiculturalwww.html | April-99 | Connie/Kim Wall | Connie | | |
| Secondary Education Lesson Plans | courses/education2/secondlessonplans.htm | September-98 | Vicki | Vicki | | |
| Secondary Math Education WWW Resources | courses/education2/math.htm | February-98 | Carolyn | Carolyn | | |
| WWW Resources for Teachers | courses/education2/teacherwww.htm | October-98 | Joyce | Consultant Kim Wall | | |
| Teaching Reading in the Elementary School | courses/education2/reading.html | June-98 | Carolyn | Carolyn | Carolyn | Carolyn |
| Young Adult Literature Sources | courses/education2/yalit.htm | April-99 | MEK | MEK | | |
| Young Adult Literature WWW Resources | courses/education2/youth.htm | October-98 | MEK | MEK | | |
| **English Composition** | | | | | | |
| Both Sides of the Issue | courses/education2/youth.htm | Oct-98 | Connie/Vicki | Connie/Vicki | | |
| Choosing a Topic | courses/english/topic.htm | Aug-98 | Frank | Frank | | |
| Hot Paper Topics | courses/english2/termindex.htm | Dec-98 | Tom/Vicki | Vicki | Vicki | |
| Research Tutorial | courses/english/research.html | Dec-97 | Team | Team | | |
| English Composition Worksheet | Microsoft word attachment | Jan-98 | Connie/Joyce | Connie/Joyce | | |
| **Evaluation of WWW Resources** | | | | | | |
| Evaluating WWW Resources | search/evaluate.htm | December-97 | Connie/Gary/Pat | Connie | Connie | Connie |

| Resource | File Name | Date | | | | | |
|---|---|---|---|---|---|---|---|
| Evaluating Web Sites | search/evaluate.htm | September-98 | Carolyn | | | | |
| Separating Myth from Reality | Power Point | | Carolyn | Connie/Gary/Frank | Carolyn | | |
| **Financial Aid** | | | | | | | |
| College Choice and Financial Aid Sources | courses/finaid/COLLEGE.HTM | Summer-96 | Connie/Vicki | Connie/Vicki | Connie/Vicki | Connie/Vicki | Connie/Vicki |
| College Choice, Scholarships & financial Aid WWW Resources | courses/finaid/collegechoice.htm | Fall-97 | Vicki | Vicki | Vicki | Vicki | Vicki |
| **Freshman Seminar** | | | | | | | |
| Owens Library Success Guide | success/successguide.html | June-97 | Team | Joyce | Joyce | Joyce | Joyce |
| Owens Library Freshman Seminar Web Page | courses/freshman/freshmanseminar.html | July-96 | Team | Connie | Connie | Connie | Connie |
| **Fundamentals of Oral Communication** | | | | | | | |
| Both Sides of the Issue | courses/speech/procon.html | October-98 | Connie/Vicki | Connie | Connie | Connie | Connie |
| Finding Periodical Articles in EBSCOhost | courses/speech/ebscohostworksheet.htm | September-97 | Connie/Carolyn | Connie | | | |
| Finding Periodical Articles in SearchBank | courses/speech/searchbankworksheet.htm | September-97 | Connie/Carolyn | Connie | | | |
| Hot Paper Topics | courses/english2/termindex.htm | Dec-98 | Tom/Vicki | Vicki | Vicki | Vicki | Vicki |
| **Geography** | | | | | | | |
| Geography WWW Resources | courses/geography/geographylinkswww.htm | Dec-98 | Pat | Pat | | | |
| **Government** | | | | | | | |
| Both Sides of the Issue | courses/speech/procon.html | October-98 | Connie/Vicki | Connie | Connie | Connie | Connie |
| How A Bill Becomes A Law | courses/billtolaw.htm | September-98 | Joyce | Joyce | Joyce | Joyce | Joyce |
| US Supreme Court Cases | courses/supctcases.htm | September-98 | Joyce | Joyce | Joyce | Joyce | Joyce |
| WWW Government Resources | government/govdoc.htm | April-98 | Sara | Sara | Sara | | |
| US Supreme Court Digest Guide | courses/government/supctdigest.htm | September-98 | Joyce | Joyce | Joyce | | |
| US Law Week Guide | courses/government/uslaw.htm | September-98 | Joyce | Joyce | Joyce | | |
| **History** | | | | | | | |
| Historical Research Guide | courses/history/research.html | February-98 | Connie | Connie | Connie | | |
| United States History Sources | courses/history/history.htm | February-98 | Connie/Vicki | Connie/Vicki | Connie/Vicki | | |
| History WWW Resources | courses/history/index.html | February-98 | Connie | Connie | Connie | | |
| American Religion Research Guide | courses/religion/americanreligion.html | November-97 | Connie | Connie | Connie | | |
| Newspaper Resources Available in Owens Library | articles/newspapers.html | | | | | | |
| Discovering U.S. History | //galenet.gale.com/a/acp/db/dtcu/ | Summer-97 | Pat | Pat | | | |
| African American History WWW | courses/history/afroamericanhistory.html | February-98 | Connie | Connie | Connie | | |
| Hispanic American History WWW | courses/history/hispanicamericanhistory.html | February-98 | Connie | Connie | Connie | | |
| Native American History WWW | courses/history/nativeamericanhistory.html | February-98 | Connie | Connie | Connie | | |
| United States WWW History | courses/history/unitedstateshistory.html | February-98 | Connie | Connie | Connie | | |
| Women's History WWW | courses/history/women.html | February-98 | Connie/Vicki | Connie/Vicki | Connie/Vicki | | |

| Title | URL | Date | | | |
|---|---|---|---|---|---|
| World History WWW | courses/history/WORLDHISTORY.HTML | February-98 | Connie | Connie | |
| **HPERD** | | | | | |
| HPERD Research Guide | courses/hperd/index.htm | May-98 | Frank | Frank | |
| HPERD Sources | courses/hperd/hperdsou.htm | May-98 | Frank | Frank | |
| HPERD WWW Resources | courses/hperd/hperdwww.htm | June-96 | Frank | Frank | |
| Search for Health Lesson Plans | courses/hperd/hlesson.htm | June-98 | Frank | Frank | |
| **Human Environmental Sciences** | | | | | |
| HES Research Guide | courses/hes/hesresearch.html | February-99 | Carolyn | Carolyn | Carolyn |
| Human Environmental Sciences | | | Leigh and | Leigh and | Carolyn |
| Library Sources | courses/hes/sources.html | April-99 | Carolyn | Carolyn | Carolyn |
| HES WWW Resources | courses/hes/heswww.html | February-99 | Carolyn | Carolyn | Carolyn |
| **Intellectual Property** | | | | | |
| Intellectual Property Resources | courses/copyright/ipresources.htm | June-99 | Joyce | Joyce | |
| **International Business** | | | | | |
| World Information Sources | courses/business/world.htm | August-97 | Joyce | Joyce | |
| International Business WWW Resources | courses/business/international.html | February-98 | Joyce | Joyce | |
| **Law** | | | | | |
| How A Bill Becomes A Law | courses/government/billtolaw.htm | September-98 | Joyce | Joyce | |
| US Supreme Court Cases | courses/government/supctcases.htm | September-98 | Joyce | Joyce | |
| US Supreme Court Digest Guide | courses/government/supctdigest.htm | September-98 | Joyce | Joyce | |
| US Law Week Guide | courses/government/uslaw.htm | September-98 | Joyce | Joyce | |
| **Literature** | | | | | |
| MLA Tutorial | courses/literature/mlatutorial.html | April-98 | Carolyn/Vicki | Vicki | |
| Literary WWW Resources | courses/literature/literarywww.htm | March-98 | Carolyn | Carolyn | |
| Literature Research Guide | courses/literature/litguide.htm | November-98 | Vicki & Tom H. | Vicki | Vicki |
| Contemporary Authors Guide | courses/literature/contempoauthors.html | April-98 | Vicki | Vicki | |
| Biographical Sources About Authors Discovering Authors | courses/literature/authors.htm galenet.gale.com/a/acp/db/dama/ | March-98 | Vicki | Vicki | |
| Childrens Literature Sources | courses/education2/childlitowens.htm | November-98 | MEK | Vicki | |
| Childrens Literature WWW Sources | courses/education2/children.htm | September-98 | MEK | MEK | |
| Literary Criticism Sources in Owens | courses/literature/literarycriticism.htm | March-98 | Vicki | Vicki | |
| Drama and Theatre sources | courses/theatre/theatresources.htm | April-98 | Frank | Frank | |
| Poetry Sources in Owens Library | courses/literature/poetry.htm | March-98 | Vicki | Vicki | |
| Short Story Sources in Owens Library | courses/literature/shortstory.htm | March-98 | Vicki | Vicki | |
| Young Adult Literature Sources | courses/education2/yalit.htm | April-99 | MEK | MEK | |
| Young Adult Literature WWW Sources | courses/education2/youth.htm | October-98 | MEK | MEK | |

## Management Information Systems

| Title | URL | Date | Reviewer | Reviewer | | |
|---|---|---|---|---|---|---|
| Finding articles about MIS topics | courses/mis/articles2.html | January-99 | Connie | Connie | | |
| MIS Tools WWW Resources | courses/mis/mistools.htm | March-99 | Connie | Connie | | |
| Management Information Systems Resources | mis/mis.htm | Fall-97 | Carolyn | Carolyn | | |

## Mass Communications

| Title | URL | Date | Reviewer | Reviewer | | |
|---|---|---|---|---|---|---|
| Both Sides of the Issue | courses/speech/procon.html | October-98 | Connie/Vicki | Connie/Vicki | | |
| Hot Paper Topics | courses/english2/termindex.htm | December-98 | Tom/Vicki | Vicki | | |
| Mass Communication Periodicals Database List | courses/masscomm/periodicals.html | March-99 | Carolyn | Carolyn | Carolyn | Carolyn |
| Movie Reviews | courses/movie/movies.htm | November-97 | Joyce | Joyce | | |

## Movie Reviews

| Title | URL | Date | Reviewer | Reviewer |
|---|---|---|---|---|
| Movie Reviews | courses/movie/movies.htm | November-97 | Joyce | Joyce |

## Music

| Title | URL | Date | Reviewer | Reviewer |
|---|---|---|---|---|
| Music Research Guide | courses/music/index.htm | November-98 | Frank | Frank |
| Music Sources | courses/music/musicsource.htm | November-98 | Frank | Frank |
| Music WWW Resources | courses/music/musicwww.htm | November-97 | Frank | Frank |

## Newspapers

| Title | URL | Date | Reviewer | Reviewer |
|---|---|---|---|---|
| Newspaper Resources Available in Owens Library | articles/newspapers.html | Summer-97 | Pat | Pat |
| Online Searchable Newspaper Sites | articles/newssites.htm | Fall-97 | Joyce | Joyce |

## Philosophy

| Title | URL | Date | Reviewer | Reviewer |
|---|---|---|---|---|
| Philosophy Research Guide | courses/philosophy/index.html | February-98 | Connie | Connie |
| Selected Philosophy Sources | courses/philosophy/bibliography.html | February-98 | Connie | Connie |
| Philosophy WWW Resources | courses/philosophy/philosophy.html | February-98 | Connie | Connie |

## Psychology

| Title | URL | Date | Reviewer | Reviewer |
|---|---|---|---|---|
| Psychology Research Guide | courses/psychology/index.htm | May-98 | Frank | Frank |
| Psychology Sources | courses/psychology/psychsources.htm | March-98 | Frank | Frank |
| Psychology WWW Resources | courses/psychology/psychwww.htm | March-98 | Frank | Frank |

## Religion

| Title | URL | Date | Reviewer | Reviewer |
|---|---|---|---|---|
| Religious Research Guide | courses/religion/religionresearch.html | November-97 | Connie/MEK | Connie/MEK |
| Religion Sources | courses/religion/religionbibliography.html | November-97 | Connie/MEK | Connie/MEK |
| Religion WWW Sources | courses/religion/religionwww.html | November-97 | Connie | Connie |
| American Religion Research Guide | courses/religion/americanreligion.html | November-97 | Connie | Connie |

## Science

| Title | URL | Date | Reviewer | Reviewer |
|---|---|---|---|---|
| Discovering Science | galenet.gale.com/a/acp/db/dtcc/ | | | |

## Statistics

| Title | URL | Date | Reviewer | Reviewer |
|---|---|---|---|---|
| Statistics Sources | courses/business/statistics.htm | August-97 | Joyce | Joyce |
| Statistics WWW Resources | courses/business/statisticswww.html | August-98 | Joyce | Joyce |

## Tax Accounting

| Item | File / URL | Date | Author | |
|---|---|---|---|---|
| Checkpoint | www.checkpoint.riag.com/ | | | |
| **Theatre** | | | | |
| Drama and Theatre Research Guide | courses/theatre/index.htm | April-98 | Frank | Frank |
| Drama and Theatre Sources | courses/theatre/theatresources.htm | April-98 | Frank | Frank |
| Drama and Theatre WWW Resources | courses/theatre/theatrewww.htm | April-98 | Frank | Frank |
| Theatre Appreciation | courses/theatre/appreciation.htm | August-97 | Frank | Frank |
| **Upward Bound** | | | | |
| Upward Bound Research Instructions | word document | | | |
| Suggested Search Terms | word document | | | |
| **Upward Bound Math/Science** | | | | |
| Career Assignment Front End | ~ubms/mathscience/ubmscareer.htm | May-99 | Frank/Connie | |
| How to Publish and Cite | ~ubms/mathscience/howdoi.htm | May-99 | Frank/Connie | |
| **Using Computers** | | | | |
| Evaluating Web Sites | courses/usingcomputers/eval.html | September-98 | Carolyn | Carolyn |
| Netscape Navigator Tutorial | ~m500627/internet/ | | Connie/Gary/Frank | |
| Owens Library Catalog and Web Pages Tutorial | courses/usingcomputers/catalog/index.html | March-98 | Frank | |
| Owens Library SearchBank Tutorial Introduction | courses/usingcomputers/searchbank/index.htm | March-97 | Connie/Gary/Frank | |
| Using Computers Curriculum Survey | courses/usingcomputers/survey/surveytext.html | November-98 | Info Team | Connie/Joyce |
| **World Wide Web Development** | | | | |
| Exploring a comprehensive course integrated ... | ??? | | | |
| **Women's Issues** | | | | |
| Women's Issues WWW Resources | courses/women/women.html | April-98 | Carolyn | |
| **GOVERNMENT INFORMATION** | | | | |
| WWW Government Resources | government/govdoc.htm | Spring-98 | Sara Duff | |
| **LIBRARY CATALOG** | | | | |
| Search the Owens Library Catalog | catalog/owens.htm | September-96 | Frank | Frank |
| Search by Author | catalog/author.htm | August-97 | Frank | Frank... |
| Search by Title | catalog/title.htm | August-97 | Frank | Frank |
| Search by Subject | catalog/subject.htm | August-97 | Frank | Frank |
| Search by Keyword | catalog/word.htm | August-97 | Frank | Frank |
| Search by Call Number | catalog/calnum.htm | August-97 | Frank | Frank |
| Frequently Asked Questions | catalog/faq.htm | | Carolyn | Consultant |

## REFERENCE RESOURCES

| Item | Path | Date | | |
|---|---|---|---|---|
| Reference Resources | ref/refdesk.htm | Summer-96 | Info Team | Connie |

## SEARCH FOR ARTICLES

| Item | Path | Date | | |
|---|---|---|---|---|
| Search for Articles | articles/webindex.htm | September-98 | Connie | Connie |
| ERIC Simple Search Guide | articles/ericguide.html | September-98 | Carolyn | Carolyn |
| Descriptions of Indexes/Databases | /articles/descript.html | July-98 | Carolyn | Carolyn |
| Find the Subject Database You Need Locating Peer-Reviewed (Refeered) | articles/databases.htm | November-97 | Carolyn | Carolyn |
| Periodicals | articles/locating.html | January-99 | Carolyn | Carolyn |
| Types of Periodicals | articles/types.html | September-98 | Carolyn | Carolyn |

## SEARCH THE INTERNET

| Item | Path | Date | | |
|---|---|---|---|---|
| Search for Specific Needs | /search/NEEDSEARCH.HTM | June-96 | Connie | Connie |
| Search Engine Tips & Tricks | search/tips.htm | Summer 96 | Info Team | Frank |

## ABOUT US
## ABOUT OWENS LIBRARY

| Item | Path | Date | | |
|---|---|---|---|---|
| About Owens Library | owens/aboutus.html | Summer 96 | Joyce | Joyce |
| Description | owens/DESCRIPT.HTM | Summer-96 | Dr. Patt | Consultant |
| Staff Directory | owens/directory.htm | Summer-96 | Pat | Pat |
| Library Floor Maps | maps/mapsmenu.html | August-97 | Pat | Pat |
| First Floor Map | maps/first.html | August-97 | Pat | Pat |
| Second Floor Map | maps/second.html | August-97 | Pat | Pat |
| Third Floor Map | maps/third.html | August-97 | Pat | Pat |
| Key Quality Indicators | owens/vision.htm | Summer-96 | Dr. Patt | Consultant |
| Library Locations | owens/locations.htm | September-97 | Pat | Pat |
| Services | services/services.htm | September-96 | Joyce | Joyce |
| Academic Computing | services/acadcom.htm | September-96 | Academic Computing Staff | Joyce |
| Circulation | services/circ.htm | September-96 | Access Services | Vicki |
| Faculty Office Calls | services/officecalls.htm | November-97 | Carolyn | Carolyn |
| Government Documents | services/govdoc.htm | September-96 | Madonna | Joyce |
| Interlibrary Loan | services/ill.htm | September-96 | Glenn | Joyce |
| Periodicals | services/periodicals.htm | September-96 | Vickey | Joyce |
| Reference | services/reference.htm | September-96 | Frank | Frank |
| Reserve | services/reserve.htm | September-96 | Vicki | Vicki |
| Student Research Consultations | services/paper.htm | September-96 | Joyce | Joyce |
| Teaching Resources Area | services/teachrsc.htm | September-96 | Sharon | Joyce |

| | | Date | | | |
|---|---|---|---|---|---|
| **Special Collections** | owens/special.htm | Summer-98 | Cathy | | |
| **Teams** | | | | | |
| Library Teams and Study Groups | owens/teams.htm | Summer-96 | Pat | Pat | |
| **Vision Statement** | owens/vision.htm#vision | Summer-96 | Dr Patt | Pat | |
| **Web Publishing Standards** | owens/guidelines/standards.htm | February-98 | Consultant | Consultant | Consultant |
| Web Page Additions and Withdrawals | owens/guidelines/webpage.htm | July-98 | Joyce | Vicki | |
| Annotation Writing | owens/guidelines/annotation.htm | August-98 | Frank | Frank | Frank |
| Content Guidelines | owens/guidelines/content.htm | August-98 | Frank | Frank | Frank |
| Content Guidelines: Copyright | owens/guidelines/copyright.htm | August-98 | Frank | Frank | Frank |
| Files and Folders | owens/guidelines/File.htm | October-98 | Frank | Frank | |
| Implementation Process | owens/guidelines/approval.htm | August-98 | Frank | Frank | |
| Resources for Web Authors | owens/guidelines/resources.htm | February-98 | Frank | Frank | Frank |
| Content Guidelines:Selection | owens/guidelines/selection.htm | August-98 | Frank | Frank | |
| Templates | owens/guidelines/template.htm | February-98 | Frank | Frank | Frank |
| Templates: Second Level, No Comments | owens/guidelines/tempsecond.htm | August-98 | Frank | Frank | Frank |
| Templates: Third Level and Underpages, No Comments | owens/guidelines/tempthird.htm | August-98 | Frank | Frank | Frank |
| Web Page Maintenance Schedule | Excel documenet | July-98 | Vicki | Vicki | |
| Web Partners | owens/guidelines/partners.htm | August-98 | Frank | Frank | |
| **What's New** | owens/whatsnew.html | January-99 | Carolyn | Carolyn | Carolyn |
| **Search These Pages** | engine/libral/index.html# | July-98 | Carolyn | Carolyn | Carolyn |

1881